Statistical Analysis with Swift

Data Sets, Statistical Models, and Predictions on Apple Platforms

Jimmy Andersson

Apress®

Statistical Analysis with Swift: Data Sets, Statistical Models, and Predictions on Apple Platforms

Jimmy Andersson
Västra Frölunda, Sweden

ISBN-13 (pbk): 978-1-4842-7764-5   ISBN-13 (electronic): 978-1-4842-7765-2
https://doi.org/10.1007/978-1-4842-7765-2

Managing Director, Apress Media LLC: Welmoed Spahr
Acquisitions Editor: Aaron Black
Development Editor: James Markham
Coordinating Editor: Jessica Vakili

Distributed to the book trade worldwide by Springer Science+Business Media New York, 233 Spring Street, 6th Floor, New York, NY 10013. Phone 1-800-SPRINGER, fax (201) 348-4505, e-mail orders-ny@springer-sbm.com, or visit www.springeronline.com. Apress Media, LLC is a California LLC and the sole member (owner) is Springer Science + Business Media Finance Inc (SSBM Finance Inc). SSBM Finance Inc is a **Delaware** corporation.

For information on translations, please e-mail booktranslations@springernature.com; for reprint, paperback, or audio rights, please e-mail bookpermissions@springernature.com.

Apress titles may be purchased in bulk for academic, corporate, or promotional use. eBook versions and licenses are also available for most titles. For more information, reference our Print and eBook Bulk Sales web page at http://www.apress.com/bulk-sales.

Any source code or other supplementary material referenced by the author in this book is available to readers on GitHub via the book's product page, located at www.apress.com/ 978-1-4842-7764-5. For more detailed information, please visit http://www.apress.com/ source-code.

Printed on acid-free paper

Table of Contents

About the Author ix

About the Technical Reviewer xi

Acknowledgments xiii

Chapter 1: Swift Primer 1

  A Swift Overview...1

    Performance...2

    Safety 2

    Correctness 3

    Hardware Acceleration 4

    Swift Package Manager 4

    Conclusion 5

  Working with Swift...5

    Data Formats 5

    The Code Project 7

    The Decodable Protocol..7

    The KeyPath Type 10

    Higher-Order Functions 14

  Chapter Summary...17

Chapter 2: Introduction to Probability and Random Variables 19

  Probability...19

    Sample Spaces...21

    Events..22

The General Addition Rule 23

Conditional Probabilities..27

Independence...31

Bayes' Theorem...31

Random Variables 34

Discrete vs. Continuous Random Variables 35

Chapter Summary 37

Chapter 3: Distributions...39

What Is a Distribution?...39

Discrete Distributions..41

Bernoulli Distribution and Trials..41

Geometric Distribution..43

Binomial Distribution 49

Distributions Application...53

Continuous Distributions...55

Differences from Discrete Distributions 55

Exponential Distribution 59

Normal Distribution 62

Expected Value 67

Variance and Standard Deviation 68

Chapter Summary 69

Chapter 4: Predicting House Sale Prices with Linear Regression 71

Linear Regression 71

Splines...73

Regression Techniques..75

Loss Function 76

Finding an Optimal Solution 79

Implementing Simple Linear Regression...81

Multiple Linear Regression...86

Deriving Linear Regression with Vectors..87

Implementing Multiple Linear Regression..91

Predicting House Sale Prices 107

Chapter Summary 107

Chapter 5: Hypothesis Testing 109

What Is Hypothesis Testing? 109

Formulating Hypotheses 110

The Null Hypothesis...111

The Alternative Hypothesis 111

Tails 112

Distribution of Sample Means..114

The Central Limit Theorem 117

Testing the Hypothesis..123

Determining Confidence Levels..123

Determining Alpha Values..124

Performing the Test 124

Determining the P-value...126

Standardization 129

Computing a Standard Score..130

Computing Confidence Intervals...132

A Word on Chi-Squared Tests...134

Chapter Summary 134

Chapter 6: Statistical Methods for Data Compression......................135

An Introduction to Compression...135

    Function Behaviors..136

    Lossless vs. Lossy Compression 139

Huffman Coding 141

    Storing the Huffman Tree..144

Implementing a Compression Algorithm..145

    The Compression Stage..145

    The Decompression Stage...158

Chapter Summary 165

Chapter 7: Statistical Methods in Recommender Systems 167

Recommender Systems 167

    The Functions of Recommender Systems 168

Approaching the Problem 169

    First Approach 169

    Second Approach..170

    Final Approach...171

Similarity Measures 173

    Cosine Similarity..173

    Euclidean Squared Distance...176

Expected Ratings 178

    Laplace Smoothing...179

    Rating Probabilities 183

Implementing the Algorithm..185

    The Main Program 186

Chapter Summary 198

Chapter 8: Reflections **199**

The Swift Programming Language 199

Probability Theory 201

Distributions...202

Regression Techniques 203

Hypothesis Testing..204

Statistical Methods for Data Compression...................................205

Statistical Methods in Recommender Systems 207

Professional Areas of Application..208

    Data Scientist 208

    Machine Learning Engineer...208

    Data Engineer 208

    Data Analyst...209

Topics for Further Studies...209

    Numerical Linear Algebra 209

    Multivariate Statistics...210

    Supervised Machine Learning 210

Index...**211**

About the Author

Jimmy Andersson is a Swedish software engineer with a flair for Swift development. During the day, he works toward a master's degree in data science and artificial intelligence at Chalmers University of Technology. At night, he builds data collection and visualization tools for the automotive industry. Jimmy also authors the open source library StatKit, which is a collection of statistical analysis tools for Swift developers.

About the Technical Reviewer

Vishwesh Ravi Shrimali graduated in 2018 from BITS Pilani, where he studied mechanical engineering. Since then, he has worked with BigVision LLC on deep learning and computer vision and was involved in creating official OpenCV AI courses. Currently, he is working at Mercedes Benz Research and Development India Pvt. Ltd. He has a keen interest in programming and AI and has applied that interest in mechanical engineering projects. He has also written multiple blogs on OpenCV and deep learning on LearnOpenCV, a leading blog on computer vision. He has also coauthored *Machine Learning for OpenCV 4* (Second Edition) by Packt. When he is not writing blogs or working on projects, he likes to go on long walks or play his acoustic guitar.

Acknowledgments

First and foremost, I would like to thank my partner Lisette for keeping me on track while writing and making sure I did not overwork myself in all the excitement. Your support and encouragement mean the world to me.

I would also like to thank the team at Apress. You have made this a fantastic journey. Thank you, Aaron, for reaching out and suggesting that we write this book; I am very grateful for the opportunity. Thank you, Jessica, for ensuring a smooth writing process and making it an enjoyable experience from start to finish. Thank you, Vishwesh, for keeping me on my toes and ensuring that the topics were relevant and correct. All help you have provided has been invaluable.

Last but not least, I want to thank my friend Bastian, who has spent the past year tossing ideas about mathematics and programming back and forth with me. The knowledge and realizations from our talks have helped me a great deal when writing this.

CHAPTER 1

Swift Primer

Swift is a general-purpose programming language built using a modern approach to safety, performance, and software design patterns.

—Swift.org

Apple introduced the Swift programming language at Worldwide Developers Conference 2014, with the vision to replace other C-based languages such as C, C++, and Objective-C. Since then, Swift has grown a passionate community of developers by striving to strike the perfect balance between performance, safety, and ease of use.

A Swift Overview

Before we dive into statistical analysis, we need to ask ourselves a few questions about whether Swift is an appropriate technology choice. Other languages support these types of calculations, and many of them have excellent third-party libraries that further extend the support of their standard libraries. To convince ourselves that Swift is a well-suited tool for these tasks, let us look at some advantageous features of the language and its ecosystem.

© Jimmy Andersson 2022
J. Andersson, *Statistical Analysis with Swift*, https://doi.org/10.1007/978-1-4842-7765-2_1

Performance

One bottleneck in modern computing is that it often includes working with significant amounts of data. For example, Microsoft's Malware Classification data set is almost half a terabyte in size, while Google's Landmark Recognition data consists of more than 1.2 million data points. Processing these amounts of data requires access to powerful hardware and demands that the programming language we use is efficient.

Performance has been an important buzzword in the marketing of Swift ever since 2014. The vision to compete with C and C++ sets a high bar for speed and efficiency, and many benchmarks show that it is doing a reasonably good job of keeping up. Compared to Python, which has pretty much become the gold standard for data scientists today, benchmarks suggest that a corresponding Swift program may yield considerable speedups. Since we know that there is much data out there to process, a high-performant language is always welcome. However, large amounts of complex data put new requirements on how well our tools allow us to manipulate it safely and correctly.

Safety

Safety is a guiding star in the development of Swift. In this context, safety means that the language actively tries to protect developers from writing code that results in undefined behavior. These safety features include such simple things as encouraging the use of immutable variables. However, they also contain far more sophisticated schemes and requirements.

One of the most prominent safety measures that Swift takes is the use of the `Optional` type. If we need to express the absence of a value, we need to use an empty Optional instead of a naked null value. Some argue that this is an unnecessarily rigid construct that leads to more boilerplate code. However, this forces developers to explicitly mark instances where data could be missing and safely handle such cases.

Another important safety feature is the requirement of exclusive memory access for modifications. Imagine a scenario where two different method calls simultaneously access the same memory location. We can consider this a safe operation, so long as both methods just read the contents and move on. However, things become problematic as soon as one (or both) wants to manipulate the stored value. The final contents in the memory location will depend on which method performs their write operation last. Swift can help point out unsafe code by requiring exclusive access for modifications, therefore demanding that only a single call can sign up to modify a memory location at any time.

Correctness

As soon as we start working with large bodies of complex data, it becomes trickier to ensure that we produce correct results. We can solve many of these problems by incorporating a good portion of sound software engineering practices. However, we should also take any help offered by our development tools.

Swift takes a great deal of inspiration from the world of functional programming. Developers are actively encouraged to consider *value types* and only resort to *reference types* if reference semantics are vital. There are many reasons why we should prefer to use *value types* when possible, but we will only look at the ones that are directly beneficial to us when working with big data sets.

The first real pro of working with *value types* is that they are generally much more performant in memory allocation. Swift generally allocates *reference types* on the heap, while *value types* typically reside on the stack. There are, as always, exceptions, but this works as a good rule of thumb. The process of allocating an object on the stack requires the system to increment a pointer, which is a speedy operation. However, to allocate an object on the heap, the system needs to search that memory area for a large enough slot. This process is much slower, and it will be noticeable if we need to allocate many objects.

The second advantage is that *value types* make copies of themselves when shared between different variables. This property means we can be confident that no other variable can change the data we are currently working on behind our backs. This locality makes it much simpler to reason about our results and perform sanity checks on individual code sections. It also simplifies things as soon as we need to parallelize our work.

Hardware Acceleration

It can be incredibly beneficial to use hardware acceleration when dealing with large amounts of data. The ability to process information in parallel can speed up our programs' execution and ultimately lead to less idle time. Swift provides several frameworks that allow developers to take advantage of multiple CPU cores and the GPU.

The problems we solve in this book are mostly going to rely on the Accelerate framework, which we mainly use for its linear algebra functionalities. For those who want to dive deeper into parallel computing after reading this, the Metal framework provides access to the graphics processors and can parallelize and speed up calculations. Both of the frameworks mentioned earlier are available on every Apple computer per default. However, we may find ourselves where the system libraries are not quite enough to do the job.

Swift Package Manager

Easy access to great external libraries is an important aspect when working with any data science tasks. The task of collecting and managing such project dependencies has become much more straightforward, thanks to developments in the Swift Package Manager. This tool allows developers to, for example, include a third-party library in their project and start working with it directly.

Other tools have offered similar functionality before, two examples being Cocoapods and Carthage. However, they have never been as tightly integrated into the Xcode environment as Swift Package Manager is today. We will take advantage of this by importing libraries that help us manipulate and visualize our data.

Conclusion

Looking at the features mentioned previously, we can conclude that Swift and its ecosystem have many desirable traits when working with statistical analysis data. It is reasonable to think that the language will serve us well once we start working with it. It is also realistic to think that using Swift might benefit us in ways that would be either difficult or impossible to achieve with other tools. With these conclusions in mind, it is time to dig into some language details that we will use in this book.

Working with Swift

This section will cover a few handy concepts that will reduce friction when working with large data sets. Some of them apply to programming in general, while others are specific to how Swift works. This section also introduces the accompanying code repository. It explains the project's general structure and how to take full advantage of it while reading this book.

Data Formats

Data points can come in many different forms, and how we choose to store our information varies between cases. Aspects such as storage size, readability, and tools available to pack and unpack the information play significant roles when picking a format. Table 1-1 (on the following page) describes a few popular data formats in the Swift community.

For the examples in this book, we have chosen to store the accompanying data using CSV files. There are many reasons for this decision:

1. CSV is a lightweight format with a relatively small memory footprint.

2. CSV stores data records as lines in a simple text file, making it a very intuitive and understandable format.

3. CSV files usually only contain plain text, which yields a high degree of readability that can be beneficial in a learning context.

4. Swift Package Manager provides access to multiple libraries for reading and writing CSV files, which decreases the friction in working with them.

Table 1-1. *Some popular data formats in the Swift community*

Format	File Extension	Description
JavaScript Object Notation	.json	JSON is a human-readable semi-structured data format.
Extensible Markup Language	.xml	XML is a structured data format that has a decent level of human readability.
Comma Separated Values Files	.csv	CSV is a compact format that typically stores tabular data in a human-readable way.
Protocol Buffers	.pb, .proto	Protocol Buffers is a serialization method for structured data, which turns information into a binary format. It is very compact but not very human readable.

The Code Project

The code repository that accompanies this book contains working examples for the problems we solve in different chapters. After downloading the project (available via a GitHub link on this book's product page at apress.com), the project opens via the **StatisticalSwift. xcworkspace** file. Notice that all code examples reside in project files named according to their respective chapter numbers. To run the code from a chapter, we first need to select the correct scheme. Clicking the scheme selection button, located right next to the Run and Stop button in the top toolbar, allows us to select the correct chapter. Doing so tells Xcode which target to execute, and we can press Cmd+R or click the Run button to run our code.

The Decodable Protocol

The Swift Standard Library comes with quite a few nice features related to encoding, decoding, and manipulating data. We will make heavy use of many of these features throughout this book, but one of them will be especially important to get things going – namely, the Decodable protocol.

The Decodable protocol itself (which we show in Listing 1-1) is as simple as it is powerful. It only specifies the requirement that conforming types should implement an initializer that knows how to instantiate an object from a Decoder.

Listing 1-1. The Decodable protocol from the Swift Standard Library

```
protocol Decodable {
  init(from decoder: Decoder) throws
}
```

As we can see, the initializer takes a `Decoder`-type object as an argument. `Decoder` is another protocol implemented by types that know how to read values from a native data format. For example, a `Decoder`-type could take a CSV file, read the lines and data values, and then provide those to a `Decodable` initializer to create new Swift objects. To get an intuition for how this works in practice, we will walk through how to decode a small CSV file step by step. Listing 1-2 shows an example CSV file containing some information about two people – Anna and Keith – while Listing 1-3 shows a Swift type named `Person`, which we would like to use to store the decoded values.

Listing 1-2. The CSV file we use in our Decodable walkthrough

```
name,age
Anna,34
Keith,36
```

Listing 1-3. The Swift type we use to showcase the functionality of the Decodable protocol

```
struct Person: Decodable {
  let name: String
  let age: Int

  enum CodingKeys: String, CodingKey {
    case name = "name"
    case age = "age"
  }

  init(from decoder: Decoder) throws {
    let container = try decoder
      .container(keyedBy: CodingKeys.self)
    self.name = try container
      .decode(String.self, forKey: .name)
```

```
    self.age = try container
      .decode(Int.self, forKey: .age)
  }
}
```

Looking at the Person type, we see that it specifies conformance to Decodable. To comply with the protocol requirements, we define the initializer and ask the Decoder to unpack the values we want to use. We also define an enum named CodingKeys, which provides a mapping between which values we ask for and their corresponding keys in the CSV. By doing so, we tell the Decoder which keys to use when we ask for different values.

Note   In many cases, we will not have to implement the initializer and CodingKeys enum from Listing 1-3. Swift can synthesize these for us if our struct only contains other Decodable types and have the same names as the data file keys.

Now that our Person type implements all the necessary functionality, we are ready to decode the data. Listing 1-4 shows the code that turns the CSV file into Person objects. One thing to be aware of is that the CSVDecoder is not a part of the Swift Standard Library. It is part of a package called *CodableCSV*, which we will introduce later.

Listing 1-4. Decoding a CSV and creating an array of Person structs

```
let decoder = CSVDecoder { config in
  config.headerStrategy = .firstLine
}

let people = try decoder
  .decode([Person].self, from: csvFile)
```

```
for person in people {
  print(person)
}

// Prints:
// Person(name: "Anna", age: 34)
// Person(name: "Keith", age: 36)
```

The code in Listing 1-4 shows the beauty of Decodable in all its glory. We turn a data file into easy-to-use Swift types by telling the CSVDecoder which data to parse and which type we expect to get back. However, statistical analysis is not just about reading files from disk. Now that we know how to load data from files, we will use the DataLoader type to read data into memory. Not only does this relieve us of the responsibilities to locate data files and handle boilerplate code, but it also allows us to focus on our primary task – to learn statistical analysis concepts. The DataLoader will be introduced in the following examples as we look at how to access and manipulate loaded data in Swift.

The KeyPath Type

One of the most powerful features in Swift's Standard Library is the KeyPath type. It gives developers the possibility to access object properties dynamically at runtime, and it does this without giving up on type safety. In this section, we will look at a few code examples. We explore what the KeyPath type is and how to leverage it to write flexible and maintainable code.

First, let us look at how we use a KeyPath to access an object property. Listing 1-5 on the following page shows an example of a KeyPath printing every Person object's name. It also introduces the use of DataLoader, which is part of the StatisticalSwift module. To get an array of all people from our data set, we call the load(_:from:) method and specify the type we expect to get back.

Listing 1-5. Using a KeyPath to print names from the people CSV file

```swift
let people = DataLoader.load(
  Person.self,
  from: .people
)

let nameKey = \Person.name
for person in people {
  let name = person[keyPath: nameKey]
  print("Name: \(name)")
}

// Prints:
// Name: Anna
// Name: Keith
```

We use the \ operator followed by the property we want to reference to create a KeyPath instance. The type of our new instance is KeyPath<Person, String>, which simply points out that we are referring to a String property stored inside a Person object. This particular example adds little to no value above the familiar dot syntax. Instead, it aims at introducing the type and its most basic use case. To explore a more practical (and arguably more realistic) use case, take a look at Listing 1-6 on the next page.

Listing 1-6. Using KeyPaths to perform data transformations

```swift
let names = people
  .map(\.name)
  .joined(separator: " and ")

let ages = people
  .map(\.age)
  .map(String.init)
  .joined(separator: " and ")
```

```
let totalAge = people
  .sum(over: \.age)

print(
    """

  We have \(names) with us today!
  They are aged \(ages), respectively,
  totaling \(totalAge) years together!
    """
)

// Prints:
// We have Anna and Keith with us today!
// They are aged 34 and 36, respectively,
// totaling 70 years together!
```

In this example, the KeyPath type transforms the different properties into new data types. KeyPath maps the corresponding property values into arrays when creating the names and ages variables, which can then be further processed and formatted into String objects. Note that this example uses implicit member syntax to reference a property. As long as the compiler can infer that we are working with the Person type, we can use the \.name shorthand instead of \Person.name to reference the name property.

The totalAge variable provides a slightly more complex and interesting use case. The method sum(over:) is from the StatKit module and does not require the KeyPath to reference a property of a specific type. Instead, it requires the reference type to conform to the AdditiveArithmetic protocol. That means that we are free to point to any property, so long as the type stored in that property supports the use of the + operator.

Lastly, we take a quick look at PartialKeyPath. This type pushes the dynamic behavior to its limits, as it does not place any requirements on the referenced property. This feature makes it possible to write highly flexible code so long as we can perform our intended operations on a type-erased object. Listing 1-7 shows an example of this.

Listing 1-7. Using partially type-erased KeyPaths to print a randomly sampled property of a Person object

```
let partialkeys: [PartialKeyPath<Person>] = [
  \Person.name,
  \Person.age
]

for _ in 1 ... 5 {
  guard
    let randomKey = partialkeys.randomElement(),
    let person = people.randomElement()
  else { continue }

  let value = person[keyPath: randomKey]
  print(value)
}
// Prints 5 random property values,
// for example Anna, Keith, or 36
```

These examples have shown some possible uses of different KeyPath types. When we start implementing solutions to the problems posed later in this book, we will notice how well this type fits into the workflow and how it allows us to alter our computations easily. Next, it has come time to cover a topic that we have already seen traces of in the previous examples and need to understand before diving into implementations.

Higher-Order Functions

When setting up data transformation pipelines, it is often helpful to make use of higher-order functions. A higher-order function is a function that does at least one of the following:

- It takes one or more other functions as input.

- It returns another function as output.

As previously mentioned, we have used higher-order functions in some examples already. In Listing 1-4, we passed a trailing closure (i.e., a function) into the initializer of the CSVDecoder to configure the parsing strategy. In Listing 1-6, we used the map(_:) method to transform some of our data using a KeyPath.

Higher-order functions are common in Swift's Standard Library and third-party libraries. Many of us may have probably used them without even realizing it. Beyond map(_:), the Swift Standard Library also provides filter(_:), reduce(_:_:), and sorted(by:), just to name a few. To get a firm grasp on how these methods operate, we will implement a new higher-order function as an extension of the MutableCollection protocol. Doing so will allow us to see what happens under the hood and understand how powerful higher-order functions can be when manipulating data.

Our higher-order function is named apply(to:_:). The concept is relatively simple – for every data point in a data set, it computes a transformation and writes back the value into the data point. One could use such methods to tidy up or polish a data set on the fly before sending it through a pipeline of statistical calculations. Such operations could, for example, include rescaling, quantization, or normalization of numerical data. Listing 1-8 shows an implementation of this function and an example of how to use it.

Listing 1-8. An implementation of the higher-order function apply(to:_:)

```swift
extension MutableCollection {
  mutating func apply<T>(
    to key: WritableKeyPath<Element, T>,
    _ transform: (T) -> T
  ) {
    for index in self.indices {
      let newValue = transform(
        self[index][keyPath: key]
      )
      self[index][keyPath: key] = newValue
    }
  }
}

var points = [
  CGPoint(x: 1, y: 1),
  CGPoint(x: 2, y: 2),
  CGPoint(x: 3, y: 3)
]

print("Before: \(points)")
points.apply(to: \.y) { value in
  value * value
}
print("After:  \(points)")

// Prints:
// Before: [(1.0, 1.0), (2.0, 2.0), (3.0, 3.0)]
// After:  [(1.0, 1.0), (2.0, 4.0), (3.0, 9.0)]
```

The code in Listing 1-8 is quite complex. Let us briefly walk through some of the critical sections to understand what is happening:

- We make the extension on the `MutableCollection` protocol. Doing so makes this implementation available on every collection type that supports mutation. This propagation of functionality is thanks to the protocol-oriented nature of Swift, but we will not cover that mechanism further in this book.

- The method `apply(to:_:)` takes two arguments. The first one is a KeyPath type which can reference any generic property of a data element. This particular type of KeyPath also supports write operations, and not just reads.

- The second argument is another function. It uses the generic type T both as input and output, which is the same T that the KeyPath references. This function should transform a data property's current value into some new value that is simpler to use or more appropriate for other calculations.

- In the method body, `apply(to:_:)` iterates over all data points in the collection. It applies the transformation function and writes back the new value to the data set. When we return, the data set no longer contains the old values but includes the specified transformations. It is notable that `apply(to:_:)` knows nothing about how to transform the values. The developer specifies that function at the call site, which makes this a very versatile approach.

There are, of course, many more subtle things going on in this function, and we could probably spend a whole other chapter talking about them. However, these few pointers should be enough to pick up on the main ideas we want to convey. Higher-order functions are powerful tools that provide highly customizable ways of manipulating data, and we will use them frequently throughout the problems we solve here.

Chapter Summary

This chapter has investigated whether or not Swift is an appropriate language for statistical analysis problems. We looked at the ecosystem surrounding the language and how well it accommodates our needs when working with such tasks. After some discussion, we concluded that Swift as a language provides many features that we would like to use when working with statistical analysis. ·

We have also looked at some of the details of Swift, putting extra weight on the types and concepts that are extra important for our use case. We learned how to decode data using the Decodable protocol and manipulate data points using different KeyPath types and higher-order functions. With these insights and new knowledge at our disposal, it is time to start looking at the actual subject – statistical analysis.

Note   Swift.org contains several great resources about Swift as a programming language. To learn more, visit `https://swift.org`.

CHAPTER 2

Introduction to Probability and Random Variables

Now that we have discussed the feasibility of choosing Swift as our primary tool for statistical analysis, we should brush up on the concepts of probabilities and random variables. These are fundamental building blocks of statistics, and we will use them extensively throughout this book. This chapter introduces some mathematical theory and lays the foundation on much of the notation we use when discussing problems and solutions. It also discusses other essential aspects, such as independence, variability, and conditioning. Without further ado, let us start by learning about probability.

Probability

Even though we may not think about it, probabilities are not just mathematical concepts exclusive to researchers and engineers. All of us evaluate and interpret probabilities every day. If we plan a trip to the beach this weekend and the weather forecast tells us that there is a 60% chance of rain on Saturday, we may choose to go on Sunday instead. If we hear that the traffic is horrible on our usual route to work this morning, we

© Jimmy Andersson 2022
J. Andersson, *Statistical Analysis with Swift*, https://doi.org/10.1007/978-1-4842-7765-2_2

may take our chances with a detour to get there on time. Granted, most of us probably do not perform any rigorous mathematical analysis in these situations. Instead, most of the time, we may rely on a gut feeling of what action maximizes the chances of reaching our goals. However, when push comes to shove, we are still estimating and evaluating probabilities of different outcomes.

A probability is, at its core, just a tool that helps us understand how likely an event is to happen. As we saw earlier, some may express it as a percentage by using numbers between 0 and 100. This book will work with probabilities as real-valued numbers in the range between 0 and 1, inclusively. This representation is more common in the scientific community, and it lends itself better for calculations. We describe a probability and the way it impacts an associated event as follows:

- An event is very likely to happen if it has a probability close to 1.

- Similarly, an event is very improbable if its probability is close to 0.

- An event with a probability of either 0 or 1 is determined. A probability of 0 suggests that the outcome is impossible, while 1 tells us that it is sure to happen.

To give a concrete example, we can consider the variable assignment `let myConstant = 5`. We declare the variable using the `let` keyword, which makes it immutable. We can describe `myConstant` with the following probability:

$$P[\text{myConstant} = 5] = 1$$

The notation above reads as "*the probability that myConstant is equal to 5 is 1*" and tells us that no matter how many times we look, the value of `myConstant` is sure to be 5.

However, the exciting bits of statistics and probability theory appear when we move away from the certainties. For example, what does it mean for something to have a probability of 0.3? To keep the discussions comprehensible as we move forward, we will use a simple six-sided die to make examples. Using a familiar item to display the usefulness of sometimes abstract topics will hopefully lead to a better understanding of why we benefit from talking about them.

Sample Spaces

Before estimating the probability of one or more events, it is helpful to know which ones are even available. In our six-sided die example, it is relatively easy to enumerate all possible outcomes. Doing so, we end up with the set of all integers from one through six. We call these numbers the *sample space* and denote them using the letter S, like so:

$$S = \{1,2,3,4,5,6\}$$

This particular sample space is a pretty manageable list of numbers, which is fortunate for us. However, the sample spaces of many other problems are massive, even infinite. For example, if we asked someone to pick any real-valued number they could think of, our sample space would be the set of all real numbers, which is an infinite set.

Since we know that S contains all possible outcomes for a die roll, we can also derive one of the most fundamental axioms of probability, namely, that

$$P[S] = 1$$

The equation above states that if we roll a die, it is 100% sure that the outcome is one of the sample points contained in the sample space.

Events

An *event* is a subset of sample points from the sample space. Suppose that we define E_1 as rolls where the die shows an even number; we effectively say that $E_1 = \{2, 4, 6\}$. If we also define an event E_2 to be rolls that show an odd number, we get two so-called *mutually exclusive* events. Two events are said to be mutually exclusive if they can never happen simultaneously. The reasoning is simple in our case. Since the number we roll is either even or odd and never both, E_1 and E_2 can never happen at the same time. This property lays the foundation for another probability axiom, which states that

If $\{E_1, E_2, E_3, \ldots\}$ is a collection of mutually exclusive events, then

$$P[E_1 \cup E_2 \cup E_3 \cup \ldots] = P[E_1] + P[E_2] + P[E_3] + \ldots$$

This axiom tells us that the total probability of a union of mutually exclusive events is equal to the sum of individual probabilities. Let us assume that our die is fair and that each side has an equal probability of showing on a roll. We compute the individual probabilities by dividing 1 (the probability of the entire sample space) by the number of items in the set, which yields 1/6 for each outcome. Now we define an event A such that a roll shows either one or two. Using the previous formula, we compute that the total probability of A is

$$P[A] = P[roll = 1 \cup roll = 2] = P[roll = 1] + P[roll = 2] = \frac{1}{6} + \frac{1}{6} = \frac{1}{3}$$

It is essential to note that this computation only holds under the assumption that the events are mutually exclusive. If they are not, we will need the help of another well-known rule.

Note   The ∪ operator used in the previous axiom is called the union operator. It takes two sets of items and merges them into a single set. The union of two sets contains all the original sets' elements but does not contain any duplicates.

The General Addition Rule

The General Addition Rule is a formula that is very similar to the one we just used. It helps compute the total probability for a union of events. However, it also considers that those events may not be mutually exclusive. We can express the rule as follows:

$$P[E_1 \cup E_2] = P[E_1] + P[E_2] - P[E_1 \cap E_2]$$

Let us work through an example in code to see why this formula fixes computations for overlapping events. Listing 2-1 on the following page shows the formula for the mutually exclusive events E_1 and E_2 at work. Listing 2-2, which follows directly after, shows the same formula, and the General Addition Rule, applied to two overlapping events, E_2 and E_3. The former yields an incorrect result, while the latter is correct. The events E_1, E_2, and E_3, are defined as follows:

- E_1: The roll shows a 1.

- E_2: The roll shows a 2.

- E_3: The roll shows an even number.

Listing 2-1. Computing the probability for a union of mutually exclusive events

```
let dieRolls = Array(1 ... 6)
let totalCount = Double(dieRolls.count)
let E1 = { (roll: Int) -> Bool in
  return roll == 1
}
let E2 = { (roll: Int) -> Bool in
  return roll == 2
}
let mutExUnionProb = Double(
  dieRolls.filter { roll in
    E1(roll) || E2(roll)
  }.count
) / totalCount

let E1Prob = Double(
  dieRolls.filter(E1).count
) / totalCount
let E2Prob = Double(
  dieRolls.filter(E1).count
) / totalCount

print(
  """
  Mutually Exclusive events E1 and E2:
  P[E1 || E2]:   \(mutExUnionProb)
  P[E1]:         \(E1Prob)
  P[E2]:         \(E2Prob)
  P[E1] + P[E2]: \(E1Prob + E2Prob)
  """
)
```

```
// Prints:
// Mutually Exclusive events E1 and E2:
// P[E1 || E2]:   0.3333333333333333
// P[E1]:         0.16666666666666666
// P[E2]:         0.16666666666666666
// P[E1] + P[E2]: 0.3333333333333333
```

Listing 2-2. Computing the probability of a union of overlapping events using the General Addition Rule

```
let E3 = { (roll: Int) -> Bool in
  return roll.isMultiple(of: 2)
}
let nonMutExUnionProb = Double(
  dieRolls.filter { roll in
    E2(roll) || E3(roll)
  }.count) / totalCount

let E3Prob = Double(
  dieRolls.filter(E3).count
) / totalCount

let E2andE3 = Double(
  dieRolls.filter { roll in
    E2(roll) && E3(roll)
  }.count) / totalCount

let genAddRule = E2Prob + E3Prob - E2andE3

print(
  """

  Events E2 and E3, no mutual exclusivity:
  P[E2 || E3]:    \(nonMutExUnionProb)
  P[E2]:          \(E2Prob)
```

```
    P[E3]:              \(E3Prob)
    P[E2] + P[E3]: \(E2Prob + E3Prob)
    P[E2] + P[E3] - P[E2 && E3]: \(genAddRule)
    """

)
// Prints:
// Events E2 and E3, no mutual exclusivity:
// P[E2 || E3]:   0.5
// P[E2]:         0.16666666666666666
// P[E3]:         0.5
// P[E2] + P[E3]: 0.6666666666666666
// P[E2] + P[E3] - P[E2 && E3]: 0.5
```

The reason that the formula for mutual exclusive cases fails may not be self-evident at first. We can expose the culprit by looking at the sample points captured by each event.

$$E_1 = \{1\}$$
$$E_2 = \{2\}$$
$$E_3 = \{2,4,6\}$$

Looking at E_1 and E_2, it is easy to see that these events do not have any overlapping sample points. That is, they are mutually exclusive. However, we can also see that E_2 and E_3 share a sample point, namely two. Using the formula for mutually exclusive events, we end up counting the probability of rolling a two twice! This problem is what the General Addition Rule addresses. The subtraction at the back of the formula makes sure we only count the probability of overlapping sample points once. Figure 2-1 shows a visual representation of the overlapping sets.

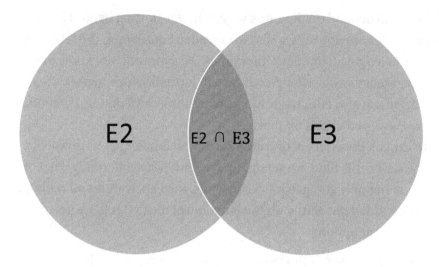

Figure 2-1. *The overlap between two events shown as a Venn diagram. The General Addition Rule compensates the overlap by subtracting the probability of elements that would otherwise be counted twice*

Now that we know the basics of sample spaces and events, we should also look at how sequences of events can depend on each other. Let us extend the die roll example to include two consecutive rolls. What is the probability that the first roll shows an even number or that the second roll shows an odd number? Similarly, how do we compute the probability that the second roll is odd, given that we roll an even number in the first throw? These are the kinds of questions we ask ourselves next.

Conditional Probabilities

There is a large body of statistical problems where an event's probability can change depending on whether another event occurs. For example, the probability of running out of fuel on the way to work will take on different values depending on whether we filled up on gas yesterday. Another example is that the probability of hitting a straight flush in a game of Texas

Hold'em will depend on the cards we get on our starting hand. These dependencies are not always easy to consider. Sometimes, the relationship can be challenging to model. Other times, we simply do not know that the dependency exists. However, if we can formalize how two events are related, we can also enrich our model with this knowledge and potentially improve any predictions we make.

To explain the concept of conditional probabilities, let us revisit our die – however, this time, we set up the preconditions differently. First of all, we are not only going to roll a single die. Instead, we start off rolling a regular, six-sided die. Based on the outcome of the first roll, we get one out of two different options:

- If the first roll shows an even number, we get to roll a second time with a die that only has even numbers on it.

- Likewise, if the first roll is odd, we get to roll another die that only has odd numbers on it.

Let us look at the different sample spaces associated with this problem. The first roll has the same sample space S that we saw before, all the integers from one through six. However, the second roll has no well-defined sample space on its own. It may be $S_2 = \{1, 3, 5\}$ or $S_2 = \{2, 4, 6\}$, depending on the outcome of the first roll. If someone were to ask us the probability that the second roll shows a two, we could not answer that with the toolkit we have used up until now. However, we could condition on the first roll and provide an answer for a particular outcome. To write down a conditional probability, we use the following notation:

$$P\left[roll_2 = 2 | roll_1 = x\right] P\left[roll_1 = x\right]$$

This equation reads as "the probability that the second roll shows a two, given that the first roll shows the number x." It highlights two important concepts. The first one is conditional probability. Since we decide that the first roll has a specific outcome x, we can also tell the probability that the second shows the number two. For example, we could tell that

$$P[roll_2 = 2|roll_1 = 1]P[roll_1 = 1] = 0$$

If we roll the number one on our first try, we cannot roll the number two on the second try according to the rules we set up.

The second important concept that is displayed here is the multiplication rule. In mathematical notation, we write this as

$$P[roll_1 = x \cap roll_2 = y] = P[roll_2 = y|roll_1 = x]P[roll_1 = x]$$

The joint probability of two events can be thought of as a multiplication of individual probabilities while considering the conditional relationship they may share. Listing 2-3 on the following page shows two code examples of conditional probability computations. The first one computes the same sequence of rolls that we did on the previous page, the second one computing the probability that a single roll is a four given that it shows an even number.

The multiplication rule is powerful for computing the joint probability of two events occurring. We have looked at examples of how to use it when investigating events that depend on each other. However, we can simplify the computations quite a lot if we can assume that they have no such relationship, which is the next section's topic.

Note   The `realValue` property used in Listing 2-3 comes from the StatKit library and does nothing more than converting a numeric type to a `Double`.

Listing 2-3. Using Swift to compute conditional probabilities

```
let dieRolls = Array(1 ... 6)
let evenRolls = [2, 4, 6]
let oddRolls = [1, 3, 5]

let firstIs1Prob = dieRolls.filter { roll in
  roll == 1
}.count.realValue / dieRolls.count.realValue

let secondIs2Prob = oddRolls.filter { roll in
  roll == 2
}.count.realValue / oddRolls.count.realValue

let rollIs4GivenEvenProb = dieRolls.filter { roll in
  roll == 4
}.count.realValue / evenRolls.count.realValue

let rollIsEven = dieRolls.filter { roll in
  roll.isMultiple(of: 2)
}.count.realValue / dieRolls.count.realValue

print(
  """
  P[roll2 == 2 | roll1 == 1]*P[roll1 == 1]:
  \(secondIs2Prob * firstIs1Prob)
  P[roll1 == 4 | roll1 == even]*P[roll1 == even]:
  \(rollIs4GivenEvenProb * rollIsEven)
  """
)
// Prints:
//P[roll2 == 2 | roll1 == 1]*P[roll1 == 1]:
// 0.0
// P[roll1 == 4 | roll1 == even]*P[roll1 == even]:
// 0.16666666666666666
```

Independence

We take out our die again, and we toss it two times without any special rules or restrictions. It is reasonable to believe that the first throw's outcome does not change our chances of hitting a specific number in the second toss. We have the same probability of throwing a two regardless of if the first roll showed a one, a six, or a four. This property is called independence, and it can significantly simplify our calculations if we can assume that it holds for the events we investigate. The multiplication rule from the previous section reduces to the following expression:

$$P[roll_1 = x \cap roll_2 = y] = P[roll_2 = y]P[roll_1 = x]$$

The second roll probability no longer depends on the first roll outcome, so we drop that conditioning. We end up multiplying the probabilities for the individual outcomes. If we wanted to calculate the probability of hitting a four in the first throw and a two in the second, we would end up with

$$P[roll_1 = 4 \cap roll_2 = 2] = P[roll_2 = 2]P[roll_1 = 4] = \frac{1}{6}\cdot\frac{1}{6} = \frac{1}{36}$$

The concepts of dependence and independence show up everywhere in statistical analysis. They can help make our models more accurate, and they can simplify mathematical expressions and logical reasoning. In the next section, we cover one of the most important theorems in statistics. It builds on conditional probabilities and allows us to extract information that would otherwise be extremely difficult to find.

Bayes' Theorem

Reverend Thomas Bayes was a statistician and Presbyterian minister in the 1700s. The theorem that bears his name deals with computing the conditional probability $P[E_1|E_2]$. The example in Listing 2-3 was quite forgiving. We were quickly able to figure out the correct value for $P[roll_1 = 4|\,roll_1 \in \{2,4,6\}]$, which allowed us to perform all of our calculations. However, there are many situations where these values are much more difficult to find. Let us explore one such situation through a toy example:

A weather station measures the temperature and presence of the sun every day. Over a year, 40% of the days have temperatures exceeding 20°C, while 50% of the days are sunny. 60% of the sunny days have temperatures that go above 20°C. If the station shows a 22°C temperature today, what is the probability that the sun shines?

We want to determine the probability of sunshine, given that it is warmer than 20°C outside. In mathematical notation, we are looking for the value of

$$P[weather = sunny|temperature > 20]$$

A quick inventory on the given information tells us that we have access to the following:

- $P[temperature > 20] = 0.4$

- $P[weather = sunny] = 0.5$

- $P[temperature > 20|weather = sunny] = 0.6$

Although the last expression is very similar to what we are interested in, it is not entirely right. However, as we are about to see, these three expressions can together provide enough information to compute the probability we want.

In the section on conditional probability, we saw that we could express the probability of two events occurring by using the following formula:

$$P[E_1 \cap E_2] = P[E_2|E_1]P[E_1]$$

However, it does not matter which event we condition on. The following "reversed" expression works equally well, as we can simply switch which event we condition on:

$$P[E_1 \cap E_2] = P[E_1 | E_2]P[E_2]$$

This realization is precisely what Bayes' Theorem utilizes. Since we now have two equations with equivalent left-hand sides, we can also equate the two right-hand sides by substitution:

$$P[E_1 | E_2]P[E_2] = P[E_2 | E_1]P[E_1] \Leftrightarrow P[E_1 | E_2] = \frac{P[E_2 | E_1]P[E_1]}{P[E_2]}$$

We have just derived Bayes' Rule, one of the most widely used formulas in statistical analysis. Returning to our weather example, we now have a way of computing the probability of interest. All we need to do is to plug our events into Bayes' Rule, which gives us the following expression (we leave out some boilerplate notation for brevity, as it is still apparent which events we talk about):

$$P[sunny | temp > 20] = \frac{P[temp > 20 | sunny]P[sunny]}{P[temp > 20]} = \frac{0.6 \cdot 0.5}{0.4} = 0.75$$

Using Bayes' Theorem, we compute a 75% chance that the sun shines given that the outdoor temperature is 22°C. This information may be more or less valuable to us, depending on whether there is a close-by window we can use to look outside. However, the same principles apply to many interesting problems, some of which we will see later in this book.

Random Variables

We have dealt with random variables earlier in this book, although we never mentioned it explicitly. For example, $roll_1$ and $roll_2$ were both random variables in our die examples. The purpose of these is to map the sample space elements to a real-valued number that we can use for computations. In the case of a die, we can already represent the number of marking of a die face as a real number, so the mapping is simply the identity function.

Other literature often denotes random variables using a single capital letter, such as X, Y, and Z. To provide a bridging foundation for further reading, we will also use this notation. In the die example, the probability of rolling a two followed by a four translates to the following notation:

$$X_1 : \textit{The first roll}$$

$$X_2 : \textit{The second roll}$$

$$P[X_1 = 2 \cap X_2 = 4] = P[X_1 = 2]P[X_2 = 4] = \frac{1}{6} \cdot \frac{1}{6} = \frac{1}{36}$$

Note that the random variable itself does not provide any information on which outcome we will actually observe if we roll the die. Even if we know that each face has a one in six chance of showing up, that does not imply that we will see each number once if we roll six times. Likewise, we cannot be sure of seeing a one even if we throw the die six times. Listing 2-4 shows a snippet of code that exemplifies this.

Listing 2-4. An example that even a fair die may not show every possible number in six throws

```
struct Die {
  func roll() -> Int {
    return .random(in: 1 ... 6)
  }
}
```

```
let die = Die()

for _ in 1 ... 5 {
  let rolls = (1 ... 5)
    .map { _ in String(die.roll()) }
    .joined(separator: ", ")

  print("We rolled \(rolls)")
}

// Prints:
// We rolled 1, 4, 4, 1, 3
// We rolled 1, 5, 6, 1, 6
// We rolled 6, 1, 6, 6, 5
// We rolled 6, 6, 4, 2, 1
// We rolled 3, 3, 2, 5, 2
```

Note   The printed die rolls in Listing 2-4 are random. That means there is a very high chance that they will differ each time the code is run.

Discrete vs. Continuous Random Variables

Another aspect of random variables ties back to their sample spaces and concerns whether they are discrete or continuous. At the beginning of this chapter, we said that a sample space encapsulates all possible experiment outcomes. We also exemplified two sample spaces, one concerning a die roll and another for asking our friend to pick any real-valued random number. The random variables associated with these experiments fall into separate categories – the die toss being a discrete random variable, while the random number picked by our friend is continuous.

To categorize a random variable as either discrete or continuous, we need to ask ourselves two questions about its sample space:

1. Is the sample space finite?

2. Is the sample space countable?

These questions may appear similar. Is countable not just another word for finite? The answer is no, and we will walk through a few examples to make it clear:

- A die has six distinct faces and, therefore, a sample space consisting of six numbers. Since the sample space holds a finite amount of numbers, and we could iterate over all of them, this is a **finite** set.

- We flip a coin and count how many times we need before it comes out tails. We could get lucky and only need one coin toss, but we could also get seriously unlucky and keep flipping coins until the end of time. The sample space consists of all the positive integers, $\{1, 2, 3, 4, ...\}$. This set is infinite since there is no limit to how high we could count. However, we can still enumerate the sample points by starting at one and going on forever. This sample space is what we call **countably infinite**.

- Asking our friend to pick a real-valued random number opens up the possibility of them choosing any number from the entire real number line, which is an infinite set. However, unlike in the previous coin flip example, this set's sample points are not countable. Not even if we restricted the choices to real numbers between 0 and 1 would the sample points be countable. We would start enumerating at 0, but then what? If we choose 0.1 next, what would happen to 0.05? The nature of the real numbers is that we can always find new values that fit between two others by adding more decimals. This property makes for an infinite and uncountable number of sample points, even between 0 and 1. We call these kinds of sets **uncountably infinite**.

Now that we know how to categorize sample spaces, we are also ready to define what it means for a random variable to be discrete or continuous:

- A random variable associated with a **finite** or **countably infinite** sample space is a **discrete** random variable.

- If the sample space of a random variable is **uncountably infinite**, the random variable is **continuous**.

The concepts of discrete and continuous will be important in the following chapters, so we must learn their definitions early on.

Chapter Summary

This chapter covered some of the most important theoretical concepts we will need in this book. We explored probabilities and their different representations, and we learned about sample spaces, events, and conditional probability. The theory we learned early in this chapter was put to good use when we discovered one of the most important theorems in statistics – namely, Bayes' Theorem. We also looked at random variables and learned how to classify them as discrete or continuous according to their sample spaces' properties.

Now that we know the basics, it is time to answer some more in-depth questions about random variables and their sample spaces. What happens if one point in the sample space is supposed to be twice as likely as the others? How do we model the likelihood of different outcomes, and how can we generate random values for a random variable where not all outcomes are equally probable? In the next chapter, we talk about distributions.

CHAPTER 3

Distributions

In the previous chapter, we discussed some characteristics of random variables. However, there is still a critical aspect of their sample spaces that we need to discuss and understand to solve problems. Returning to the die example, we know that the sample space associated with one throw contains all integer numbers from one through six. While that is helpful information, the sample space alone tells us nothing about how likely we are to roll a specific number.

Until now, we have assumed that each die face is equally probable to show, but that might not always be the case. What if someone tampered with the die, making it twice as likely that you would roll a two than any other number? How do we describe our chances of throwing an even number under those conditions? These are some of the questions we will discuss and answer in this chapter.

What Is a Distribution?

A distribution is a description of how likely the points in a sample space are. For the case of a fair die, each face is equally likely to show, and the total probability of one is distributed evenly over the six possible outcomes. We can express the distribution using the following function:

$$P[X = x] = \begin{cases} \dfrac{1}{6} & \text{if } x \in \{1,2,3,4,5,6\} \\ 0 & \text{otherwise} \end{cases}$$

© Jimmy Andersson 2022

J. Andersson, *Statistical Analysis with Swift*, https://doi.org/10.1007/978-1-4842-7765-2_3

We can also express the distribution of our fair die by using a column chart. By placing the sample points on the X axis and the relative probabilities on the Y axis, we get a diagram that looks like the one in Figure 3-1.

Figure 3-1. *The probabilities of different outcomes of a die throw*

As we discovered in the last chapter, the sample space of a die roll is discrete since it contains a finite set of sample points. We also learned that this classification extends to random variables representing a die toss, making it a *discrete random variable*. On top of that, this categorization also applies to distributions since they also describe sample spaces. The distribution of a fair die is, therefore, a *discrete distribution*. The same logic applies to *continuous distributions*, which deal with uncountably infinite sample spaces.

We spend the remainder of this chapter exploring and understanding some of the most common standard distributions, their properties and parameters, and which helpful information we can derive from them. We will use this information for further calculations in later chapters, so we must develop a good intuition for what it means as early as possible. We start by looking at discrete distributions.

Discrete Distributions

As we have covered before, the distribution of a die roll is discrete because the sample space is finite. However, we will start this section using something even cleaner and more straightforward – a coin toss!

Bernoulli Distribution and Trials

The concept of a Bernoulli trial is quite simple. We perform a single experiment, a trial, which either comes out as a success or a failure. We traditionally denote the probability of success by p and that of a failure by q. Since these events are mutually exclusive and make up the entirety of the sample space, we can describe their relationship with the following formula:

$$q = 1 - p \iff p + q = 1$$

Imagine now that we flip a coin and label heads up as a "success." That implies that we label tails up as a "failure." If the coin is fair, it will have an equal 0.5 chance of landing with either side up. The column chart of such a coin would look similar to the diagram of the die roll we saw earlier, only with two columns instead of six. Mathematically, we describe such a coin by writing

$$X \sim Bernoulli(0.5)$$

The earlier notation tells us that the random variable X (representing the coin flip outcome) is Bernoulli distributed and that

$$p = 0.5$$

$$q = 1 - p = 1 - 0.5 = 0.5$$

That is, both sides are equally likely to show when we toss the coin. However, let us look at a scenario where the coin has a slight imperfection and tends to land heads up a little more often.

Let us say that the new coin has a 0.54 probability of landing heads up and that the random variable Y represents it. Then, by the same logic as before, we would describe it by writing

$$Y \sim Bernoulli(0.54)$$

$$p = 0.54$$

$$q = 1 - p = 0.46$$

Our first thought might be that this does not make a big difference. Flipping the new coin still yields an almost 50-50 chance of landing on either side. However, if we were to flip this coin many times, we would realize that this slight bias yields a greater chance of seeing more heads than tails. We can illustrate this by writing a small toy script like in Listing 3-1, which flips 10,000 coins two times, each with different probabilities of landing heads up.

Listing 3-1. Simulating two sequences consisting of 10,000 coin flips each, one with p = 0.5 and the other with p = 0.54

```
func simulate(p: Double) {
  let q = (100 - p * 100).rounded() / 100

  let results = (1 ... 10000)
    .reduce(into: [0, 0]) { result, _ in
    let success = Double.random(in: 0 ... 1) < p
    result[success ? 1 : 0] += 1
  }
  .enumerated()
  .map { index, count in
```

```
    let outcome = (index == 0) ? "Tails" : "Heads"
    let probability = (index == 0) ? q : p
    return "\(outcome) (\(probability)): \(count)"
  }

  print(
    """

    \(results.joined(separator: "\n"))

    """

  )
}

simulate(p: 0.50)
simulate(p: 0.54)

// -- These prints may vary since we
// -- are dealing with random variables
// Prints:
// Tails (0.5): 5042
// Heads (0.5): 4958
//
// Tails (0.46): 4588
// Heads (0.54): 5412
```

Geometric Distribution

Now we know how to think about single trials with binary outcomes. However, in some situations, we may want to know something about the probability of eventual success. For example, if we start flipping a coin over and over, how likely is it that it lands heads up on the third try? Regarding the sample space, we write it as follows:

$$S = \{H, TH, TTH, TTTH, \ldots\}$$

43

The coin may land heads up on the first try, but we may also see a few tails on the way there. If we are very unlucky, we might see an infinite number of flips land tails up before we succeed. Computing the probability of each of them is no more difficult than applying the multiplication rule.

Using the notation and reasoning from the section on Bernoulli trials, the chance of succeeding on a single toss is p. To get the likelihood of making it on the second try, we consider that we need to fail the first attempt. Because each flip is independent of the others, we can calculate our result by multiplying the probabilities of failing once and succeeding once.

$$P[X = 2] = p \cdot q$$

It is possible to keep expanding this by adding more failures before our first success and multiplying their probabilities:

$$P[X = 3] = p \cdot q \cdot q = p \cdot q^2$$

$$P[X = 4] = p \cdot q \cdot q \cdot q = p \cdot q^3$$

$$P[X = 5] = p \cdot q \cdot q \cdot q \cdot q = p \cdot q^4$$

$$P[X = 6] = p \cdot q \cdot q \cdot q \cdot q \cdot q = p \cdot q^5$$

$$\dots$$

These formulas generalize nicely into a compact notation by writing

$$P[X = x] = p \cdot q^{x-1}, \ x \in \mathbb{N}^+, \ p \in (0, 1]$$

We have just derived the *probability mass function* (PMF) of the geometric distribution. The PMF gives us a formula for computing the likelihood of an outcome in a discrete distribution. The notation also tells us that x needs to be an element in the positive natural numbers and that the parameter p needs to lie in the interval $0 < p \leq 1$. Just as in the Bernoulli trial examples, we can compute the parameter q from the value of p.

Listing 3-2 on the following page shows a short program that computes the PMF of a geometric distribution with parameter $p = 0.4$. If we translate this back to the coin example, it calculates the likelihood of the first heads showing after some exact number of tries, given that our coin is slightly biased toward landing tails up. Plotting the results in a column chart, we get the diagram shown in Figure 3-2.

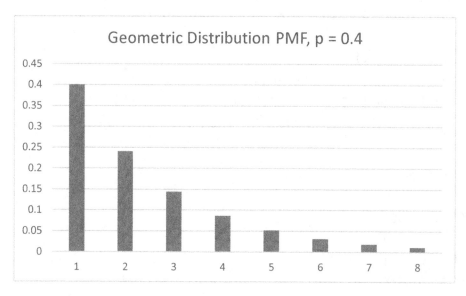

Figure 3-2. *Plotting the PMF of a geometric distribution with parameter $p = 0.4$*

Listing 3-2. Computing the probability mass function of a geometric distribution with parameter $p = 0.4$

```
import Foundation

private static func geometricPMF(
  of x: Int,
  with p: Double
) -> Double {
```

```
  precondition(0 < x, "0 ≮ x.")
  precondition(0 < p && p <= 1, "p ∉ (0, 1].")
  return p * pow(1 - p, Double(x) - 1)
}

(1 ... 8)
  .reduce(into: [Int: Double]()) { result, x in
    result[x] = geometricPMF(of: x, with: 0.4)
  }
  .sorted(by: <)
  .forEach { trials, prob in
    let probability = String(format: "%.4f", prob)
    print("\(trials): \(probability)")
  }

// Prints:
// 1: 0.4000
// 2: 0.2400
// 3: 0.1440
// 4: 0.0864
// 5: 0.0518
// 6: 0.0311
// 7: 0.0187
// 8: 0.0112
```

Note   The chart in Figure 3-2 looks very similar to the one in Figure 3-1, and it does so for a good reason. The diagram in Figure 3-1 also depicts a PMF (of a discrete uniform distribution). In fact, every discrete distribution has a PMF.

We know that the PMF gives us a way to compute the probability of a single outcome. But, what if we want to know how likely it is that we need to flip the coin at most three times before it lands heads up? To do so, we can follow a pretty straightforward train of thought:

- First, we conclude that it does not matter to this question if we succeed in one, two, or three tries. All of them satisfy our predicate and are therefore valid.

- Second, we realize that the PMF gives us a way to calculate the probability of a single outcome.

By writing down our question mathematically and using some of the rules we learned about in previous chapters, we get

$$P[X \leq 3] = P[X = 1 \cup X = 2 \cup X = 3] =$$

$$P[X = 1] + P[X = 2] + P[X = 3] = \sum_{x=1}^{3} P[X = x]$$

The second to last equality comes from the fact that the events are mutually exclusive. We can therefore sum the individual probabilities without compensating for overlaps. Finally, if we assume that the coin is fair and has a 50-50 chance of landing with either side facing up, we can expand the formula, substitute the actual values for p and q, and compute a result like so:

$$P[X \leq 3] = \sum_{x=1}^{3} P[X = x] = \sum_{x=1}^{3} p \cdot q^{x-1} =$$

$$0.5 \cdot 0.5^0 + 0.5 \cdot 0.5^1 + 0.5 \cdot 0.5^2 = 0.875$$

According to this result, a fair coin will land heads up within three flips in 87.5% of cases. Had the coin been biased, with $p = 0.3$, that probability would have been 0.657. That is quite a difference!

The function that we just derived for the geometric distribution, P[X ≤ x], is also a special one. It is called the cumulative distribution function (CDF), and it tells us how likely it is that a randomly sampled point from a distribution is less than or equal to some x. Figure 3-3 visualizes this relationship by highlighting the probabilities we summed over to arrive at a result for P[X ≤ 3].

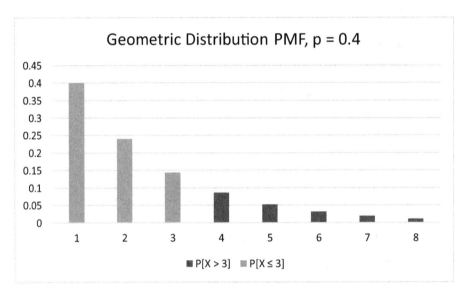

Figure 3-3. *The CDF is computed by summing over all probabilities smaller than or equal to some number. In this case, that number is 3*

In the case of the coin flip, we used it to compute the proportion of times we would need at most three flips before a toss came out heads up. Listing 3-3 shows a code snippet that calculates the probability of needing at most five coin flips, given that we use a heavily biased coin with $p = 0.25$. We see that there is only about a 76% chance of a toss landing heads up with such a strong bias, even if we flip the coin five times!

Listing 3-3. Computing the likelihood of seeing at least one head in eight coin flips using the geometric cumulative distribution function.

```
private static func geometricPMF(
  of x: Int,
  with p: Double
) -> Double {

  precondition(0 < x, "0 ≮ x.")
  precondition(0 < p && p <= 1, "p ∉ (0, 1].")
  return p * pow(1 - p, Double(x) - 1)
}

let probability = 0.25
let cdf = (1 ... 5)
  .reduce(into: 0.0) { result, x in
    result += geometricPMF(of: x, with: probability)
  }

print("P[X ≤ 5] = \(cdf)")

// Prints:
// P[X ≤ 5] = 0.7626953125
```

Binomial Distribution

Now we know how to reason about single binary events using Bernoulli trials. We also know how to make sense of sequences of Bernoulli trials that terminate on the first successful outcome. As the last step in exploring standard discrete distributions, we will ask ourselves how likely it is to get some exact number of successes on a fixed number of Bernoulli trials. For example, if we flip a coin five times, how probable is it that we see precisely three heads?

49

The first approach toward a solution may be to look at the geometric distribution for guidance. If we set up a sequence of five Bernoulli trials and three of them are successful, that implies that two were not. Using this reasoning, we could write the following:

$$P[X = 3; n = 5] = p^3 \cdot q^{5-3} = p^3 \cdot q^2$$

The preceding notation specifies that we are looking for the probability that the random variable X is equal to three, just like it did before. We also provide a fixed parameter n, which tells us how many trials we want to conduct. The p and q parameters are the same as in the sections on Bernoulli trials and geometric distributions.

To be honest, this approach is not that far off. However, it overlooks the fact that there may be many combinations that result in three successful trials. For example, if H denotes a coin landing heads up and T is tails up, we may find ourselves with any of the following combinations:

$$\{H, H, H, T, T\}$$
$$\{H, H, T, H, T\}$$
$$\{H, T, H, H, T\}$$
$$\{T, H, H, H, T\}$$
$$\{T, H, H, T, H\}$$
$$\{T, H, T, H, H\}$$

$$\cdots$$

As we can see, all of these are perfectly valid combinations of coin flips. Our formula, however, only accounts for one of these. It does not matter which one; the important thing to note is that we are not taking into our calculations that there may be multiple outcomes that satisfy our condition. In comes the binomial coefficient to the rescue.

The binomial coefficient, also known as the combinatorial number or "n-choose-k," represents the number of ways we can pick a subset of k unordered items from a set of n possible outcomes. The following equation shows the mathematical shorthand and the formula for the binomial coefficient:

$$\binom{n}{k} = \frac{n!}{k!(n-k)!} \quad , \quad k \in \{0, 1, 2, \ldots, n-1, n\}$$

Note that other formulations of the binomial coefficient allow both n and k to be real valued (or even complex). However, we will only concern ourselves with this variant for now. The proof of this formulation is beyond the scope of this book, but we will show a small example that allows us to see how it works.

If we flip three coins and want to know how many combinations exist where one of the flips lands heads up, we can list and count the possible outcomes that match our predicate, like so:

$$\{H,T,T\}, \quad \{T,H,T\}, \quad \{T,T,H\}$$

Since we are using a relatively small sample space, it is easy to verify that these three sequences are the only ones that satisfy the requirement. If we instead wanted to solve this using the binomial coefficient, we would get

$$\binom{3}{1} = \frac{3!}{1!(3-1)!} = \frac{3 \cdot 2}{2} = 3$$

This result matches the one we got from counting manually. This method may not give much of an edge for small examples such as this. However, it becomes handy as the sample spaces grow larger.

Now that we know how to compute the likelihood of a single combination of coin flips and the total number of valid combinations, we are ready to solve our initial problem. The probability of seeing three heads when flipping a coin five times boils down to multiplying these two entities:

$$P[X=3; n=5] = \binom{n}{k} \cdot p^3 \cdot q^2$$

The previous formula is the binomial distributions PMF. If we, for example, were to flip a perfectly fair coin four times, the likelihood of three landing heads up would be

$$P[X=3; n=4]=\binom{4}{3}\cdot 0.5^3 \cdot 0.5^1 = \frac{4!}{3!(4-3)!}\cdot 0.5^4 = 4\cdot 0.5^4 = 0.25$$

The binomial distribution also has a CDF. Just as with the geometric distribution, we compute it by summing up the PMFs for all outcomes less than or equal to some number:

$$P[X\leq x]=\sum_{i=0}^{x}P[X=x]=\sum_{i=0}^{x}\binom{n}{i}\cdot p^i \cdot q^{n-i}$$

The code in Listing 3-4 shows a small example of computing the PMF of a binomial distribution. The snippet borrows the function choose(n:k:) from StatKit, which calculates the combinatorial number for k successes on n trials.

Listing 3-4. Computing the binomial PMF with parameters p = 0.4 and n = 10

```
func binomialPMF(
  of x: Int,
  p: Double,
  n: Int
) -> Double {
  precondition(0 < x, "0 ≮ x.")
  precondition(0 < p && p <= 1, "p ∉ (0, 1].")
  precondition(0 < n, "n must be positive.")

  let binomialCoef = choose(n: n, k: x).realValue
  let successProb = pow(p, x.realValue)
```

```
    let failureProb = pow(1 - p, (n - x).realValue)
    return binomialCoef * successProb * failureProb
}

let p = 0.4
let n = 10
let x = 7

let pmf = binomialPMF(of: x, p: p, n: n)
let probability = String(format: "%.2f", p)

print(
    """
    Likelihood of \(x) heads,
    with p = \(probability) and n = \(n):
    \(String(format: "%.4f", pmf))
    """
)

// Prints:
// Likelihood of 7 heads,
// with p = 0.40 and n = 10:
// 0.0425
```

Distributions Application

Now that we know the basics of discrete probability distributions, it is time to introduce an outsider in the code repository. The DistributionsApp project is not quite like the other code examples that come with this book. Running this code does not produce any numeric results to the terminal but opens an interactive application like the one shown in Figure 3-4.

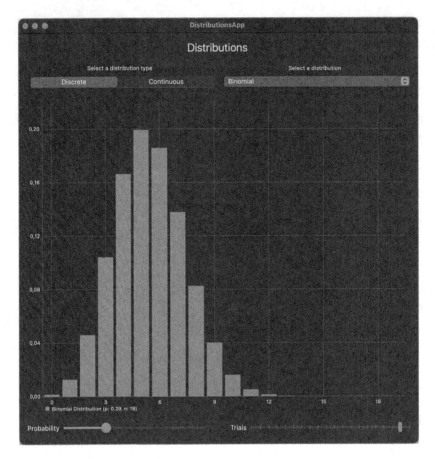

Figure 3-4. *The DistributionsApp project from the code repository*

DistributionsApp allows us to play around with the parameters of
some standard distributions, which lets us develop an intuition for how the
probabilities of different outcomes change. All we need to do to get started
is to

- Select the type of distribution we want to see from the
  segmented control to the upper left.

- Select one of the different standard distributions that
  become available in the drop-down menu to the upper
  right.

- Change the parameters of our selection using the controls that show up beneath the chart.

This application supports both discrete and continuous distributions, some of which we have covered, while others are new and may serve as inspiration for further studies. Take a few minutes to look at the different charts and study how they change while manipulating their parameters. The program will be of use as we head into the next section, covering the basics of continuous distributions.

Continuous Distributions

A continuous distribution is, conceptually, not very different from a discrete distribution. It is still a description of the likelihood of various outcomes in a sample space. However, continuous distributions are very different as soon as we start using them for computations. Some differences are easy to get used to, while others may feel downright counterintuitive when we run into them.

Differences from Discrete Distributions

One of the main areas where continuous distributions differ from discrete ones is that they do not have a probability mass function. Instead, continuous distributions have a similar property called the *probability density function* (PDF). Rather than visualizing a PDF with columns in a chart, we use a line chart that produces a curve over all sample points, like the one in Figure 3-5.

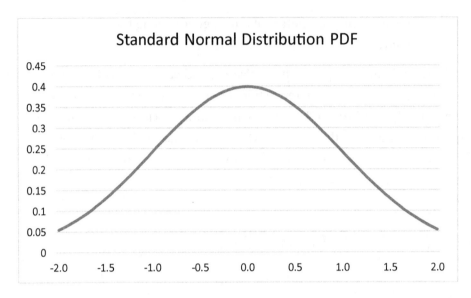

Figure 3-5. *A chart showing the PDF of a standard normal distribution*

While a continuous line certainly makes a more visually pleasing chart than the columns we saw in the discrete charts, the infinite number of sample points also makes things a bit tricky. It may not be evident at first, but the values on the Y axis no longer represent probabilities. To clarify, we list a few of the sample points in Table 3-1.

Table 3-1. *A few sample points from a standard normal distribution*

Sample Point	PDF Value
-0.10	0.397
-0.05	0.398
0.00	0.399
0.05	0.398
0.10	0.397

If we treated these values as probabilities, there would be an approximate 199% chance of sampling any of these five points from a standard normal distribution. That is not realistic given that the total probability of the entire sample space should be equal to 1 and that there is an infinite amount of other points to choose from. This realization forces us to ask what the PDF values really represent and why they are different from the PMF values.

The discrete distributions make it relatively simple to picture how the probability of all individual sample points sum to one. However, the same picture is not as simple to paint when dealing with infinitely many sample points. How small would we have to make each PDF value to make sure that they sum to one? The answer is that we do not use regular sums to make calculations with continuous distributions – we use integrals, which come with properties that may be counterintuitive or even undesirable at times.

Anyone who has taken a calculus class can testify that some integrals are incredibly complicated to compute. It is no different in statistics, where we often end up with equations containing the PDFs of multiple dependent random variables. Another surprising property of a continuous sample space is that the probability of any single point is zero. Yes, it is true. The following is a quick outline of why:

Let $f(x)$ be the PDF of a continuous random variable.

Let $F(x)$ be the primitive function of $f(x)$. Then

$$P[X=x] = \int_{x}^{x} f(x)\,dx = \left[F(x)\right]_{x}^{x} = F(x) - F(x) = 0$$

The aforementioned does not serve to be rigorous proof but rather to provide insight into why the numbers work out the way they do. The quick-and-dirty explanation is that the probability of any single sample point approaches zero as the number of sample points approaches infinity.

There are, as always, exceptions to this. However, in general, this means that we only ask questions about whether a continuous random variable is within some range of values. Figure 3-6 shows a visual representation of how the continuous CDF relates to the PDF. Computing the CDF comes down to calculating the area under the PDF curve.

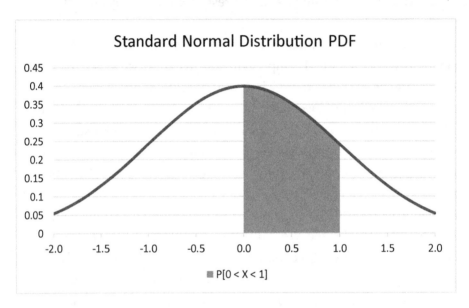

Figure 3-6. *Computing the continuous CDF comes down to calculating the area under the PDF curve. In this case, P[0 < X < 1] is highlighted*

Luckily for us, we will not have to deal with integrals a whole lot in this book. Many standard distributions have closed-form analytical solutions or approximations of their cumulative distribution functions, which we can exploit to calculate our answers instead. Now, let us continue by looking at a continuous standard distribution often used in counting processes and queueing theory.

Exponential Distribution

The exponential distribution describes the distribution of time between two events in a Poisson distribution. We did not cover the Poisson distribution specifically, but the exponential distribution is still a good tool for calculations on its own.

The exponential distribution has a single parameter, commonly referred to as the *rate*, denoted by the Greek letter λ. The rate tells us the average number of events that occur in a decided unit of time. For example, if we owned a store with an average of 20 customers visiting every day, we could let the time unit be one day, and the rate would be 20. If we instead choose one hour to be our base, the rate is two (given that the store is open for 10 hours). A good thing to note is that since we deal with time intervals, the sample space is made up strictly of nonnegative numbers.

The exponential distribution describes how likely it is that some time interval separates two events. For example, if our store has two customers visiting every hour, we could calculate the probability that the first customer arrives within 10 minutes of our opening. We could write this mathematically using the following notation:

$$P\left[\, 0 \leq X \leq \frac{1}{6}; \lambda = 2 \right]$$

Note that we need to specify a range of values since we deal with a sample space containing continuous time intervals. The probability that the first customer arrives precisely ten minutes after opening is zero, by the same reasoning that we applied in the previous section. We also note that the upper bound is not ten, but rather the fraction of our base unit (one hour) that ten minutes make up.

We could compute the integral of the exponential distribution PDF from zero through ten minutes to answer our question. The derivation of the PDF is beyond the scope of this book. Instead, we simply present the formula in the following equation:

$$P\left[0 \le X \le \frac{1}{6}; \lambda = 2\right] = \int_0^{\frac{1}{6}} \lambda e^{-\lambda x} dx = \left[-e^{-\lambda x}\right]_0^{\frac{1}{6}} = 1 - e^{-\frac{2}{6}} \approx 0.283$$

The calculation shows us that if we were to oversleep and be ten minutes late to open the store, there is an approximate 28.3% risk that our first customer shows up before us and, consequently, leaves without buying anything.

This particular integral was not that bad. It was, in fact, reasonably well behaved and easy to compute. However, there is another way to calculate the same result using the cumulative distribution function. We show the exponential distribution CDF here:

$$P[X \le x] = 1 - e^{-\lambda x}$$

This formula looks very similar to one of the last equalities in the integral we just solved. Since it calculates the probability that our random variable falls below a certain threshold, we will use it to perform a trick. If we wanted to know the likelihood of the first customer showing up in the first five to ten minutes, we could compute the integral again. However, we could also rephrase the question like

$$P\left[X \le \frac{1}{6}; \lambda = 2\right] - P\left[X \le \frac{1}{12}; \lambda = 2\right]$$

That is, we compute the likelihood of our first customer showing up within ten minutes of opening, but we subtract the probability that they show up within the first five minutes to get an answer for the range in which we are interested:

$$P\left[X \le \frac{1}{6}; \lambda = 2\right] - P\left[X \le \frac{1}{12}; \lambda = 2\right] = 1 - e^{-\frac{2}{6}} - 1 + e^{-\frac{2}{12}} \approx 0.13$$

This trick also works consistently for the first example. The only change we need to make is to subtract the probability of the first customer showing up within zero minutes instead of five. The code in Listing 3-5 shows how one could compute the likelihood of an event occurring between time x_1 and x_2, given an exponential distribution with rate λ.

Listing 3-5. An example of computing the probability of an event occurring given an exponential distribution

```
func probability(
  between x: Double,
  and y: Double,
  rate: Double
) {

  precondition(0 <= x, "x mustbe non-negative.")
  precondition(0 <= y, "y must be non-negative.")
  precondition(x <= y, "x must be ≤ y.")
  precondition(0 < rate, "rate must be positive.")

  let upperCDF = 1 - exp(-rate * y)
  let lowerCDF = 1 - exp(-rate * x)
  let prob = upperCDF - lowerCDF

  print(
    """
```

```
      P[\(x) ≤ x ≤ \(y) | λ = \(rate)] = \(prob)
      """

   )
}

probability(between: 0, and: 1, rate: 2)
probability(between: 0, and: 1, rate: 0.2)
probability(between: 0, and: 0, rate: 10)

// Prints:
// P[0.0 ≤ x ≤ 1.0 | λ = 2.0] = 0.86466471167633873
// P[0.0 ≤ x ≤ 1.0 | λ = 0.2] = 0.18126924692201818
// P[0.0 ≤ x ≤ 0.0 | λ = 10.0] = 0.0
```

Now that we have some experience working with continuous sample spaces, it is time to look at one of the most important and widely used continuous distributions.

Normal Distribution

The French mathematician Abraham de Moivre first described the normal distribution in the 1700s. The discovery went under the radar for quite some time until it was "rediscovered" by Carl Friedrich Gauss and Pierre-Simon Laplace. It is also commonly referred to as the Gaussian distribution or a bell curve because it has the general shape of a bell.

We can define a normal distribution by its mean and standard deviation. The mean, denoted by the Greek letter μ, specifies the most common value in the distribution. This value resides at the center of the curve, and the shape mirrors on each side of this point. The standard deviation, denoted by σ, describes the "wideness" of the bell. A greater value means that sample points tend to be farther away from the mean, while a smaller σ indicates that samples are usually closer to it. We will cover these concepts in greater depth later in this chapter. For now, it is enough to have a high-level intuition.

Figure 3-7 shows two normal distributions with the same parameter μ, but different σ. Notice how the σ parameter makes the mean less likely, while samples further away become much more probable. The DistributionsApp project also provides a tool to test how different parameter values change the likelihood of sample points.

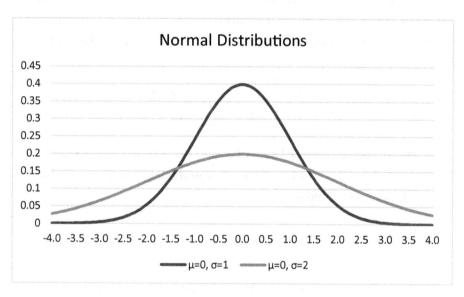

Figure 3-7. *Two normal distributions with different parameters*

To perform calculations with the normal distribution, we need to know its PDF:

$$f(x) = \frac{1}{\sigma\sqrt{2\pi}} e^{-\frac{1}{2}\left(\frac{x-\mu}{\sigma}\right)^2}$$

This formula gives us the relative likelihood value of any sample point. It is worth noting that this particular sample space contains every real number, ranging from negative infinity to positive infinity. However, to calculate the probability that a sample falls within some range, we need to compute an integral:

$$P[x_1 < X < x_2] = \int_{x_1}^{x_2} \frac{1}{\sigma\sqrt{2\pi}} e^{-\frac{1}{2}\left(\frac{x-\mu}{\sigma}\right)^2} dx$$

We realize quickly that this is a much more complex computation than the one we had to perform for the exponential distribution. Unfortunately, using the CDF and performing the same trick we did with the exponential distribution does not help us. Let us look at the function to understand why:

$$P[X < x] = \frac{1}{2}\left[1 + erf\left(\frac{x-\mu}{\sigma\sqrt{2}}\right)\right]$$

As we can see, that is one beast of a function. The normal distribution CDF relies on Gauss's error function, commonly denoted by *erf(z)*. It is a complex function defined as

$$erf(z) = \frac{2}{\sqrt{\pi}} \int_0^z e^{-t^2} dt$$

The error function also contains an integral, and it is no easier to compute than the one we saw on the previous page. Fortunately, researchers have developed ways to approximate the error function with stunning precision. *Handbook of Mathematical Functions with Formulas, Graphs, and Mathematical Tables* (1964, p. 299), written by Milton Abramovitz and Irene Stegun, contains a formula devised by Cecil Hastings Jr to approximate the error function. It has a relatively low computational cost and is easy to implement, making it very attractive for our purposes. Listing 3-6 provides an implementation, and Listing 3-7 used said implementation to approximate the normal distribution CDF.

Listing 3-6. Approximating Gauss's error function

```
import Darwin

let p = 0.3275911
let coefficients = [
  0.254829592,
  -0.284496736,
  1.421413741,
  -1.453152027,
  1.061405429
]
let exponents = (1 ... coefficients.count)
  .map(Double.init)

func erf(_ z: Double) -> Double {
  let sign = (z.sign == .plus) ? 1.0 : -1.0
  let absZ = abs(z)
  let t = 1 / (1 + p * absZ)

  let powerSeries = zip(coefficients, exponents)
    .reduce(into: 0.0) { (result, zipped) in
      let (coefficient, exponent) = zipped
      result += coefficient * pow(t, exponent)
    }

  let tail = powerSeries * exp(-pow(absZ, 2))
  return sign * (1 - tail)
}
```

Listing 3-7. Computing the normal distribution CDF with Gauss's error function approximation

```
func normalCDF(
  x: Double,
  mu: Double,
  sigma: Double
) -> Double {
  let z = (x - mu) / (sigma * sqrt(2))
  return 0.5 * (1 + erf(z))
}

print(
  """

  Standard Normal Distribution
  P[X < 0] = \(normalCDF(x: 0, mu: 0, sigma: 1))
  """
)

// Prints:
// Standard Normal Distribution
// P[X < 0] = 0.5000000005
```

The true solution to the CDF in Listing 3-7 is 0.5, while our approximation yields a result of 0.5000000005. We are okay with that error because it does not make a massive difference to the overall likelihood we are calculating. The implementation also provides the ability to calculate the probability of falling inside a specific range of values by using the same trick that we used with the exponential distribution:

$$P[x_1 < X < x_2] = P[X < x_2] - P[X < x_1]$$

Approximations usually feel cheap and dirty. However, it is something that we have to accept and embrace. Many calculations we make on a modern computer end up being approximations because of limitations in bitwidth. To be fair, many mathematical formulas that we may think of as being exact are also approximations of empirical measurements.

We now know about some of the most common standard distributions. There are, of course, many more than these. However, these concepts apply to those as well. To finish up this chapter, let us have a look at a few more properties of distributions. These will be used later in the book, and we must know what they are.

Expected Value

One of the most common uses of an expected value is what we usually refer to as an average. We define the expectation of a random variable like

$$\mathbb{E}[X] = \sum_{x \in S} x \cdot p(x) \quad \textit{for discrete distributions}$$

$$\mathbb{E}[X] = \int_{-\infty}^{\infty} x \cdot f(x)\,dx \quad \textit{for continuous distributions}$$

In these formulas, $f(x)$ is the PDF of a continuous distribution, while we use $p(x)$ to denote the PMF of a discrete distribution. The expectation of a random variable yields a real number (at least for the distributions we'll encounter in this book). This number does not have to be part of the sample space of the random variable. This fact might feel strange or counterintuitive at first, given the name. Isn't the expectation supposed to compute the expected value of a distribution?

To make this concept more tangible, we will revisit the die and compute a few expectations. We start by focusing on a fair die, which has an equal chance of landing with either face up. The expectation becomes

$$\mathbb{E}[X] = 1 \cdot \frac{1}{6} + 2 \cdot \frac{1}{6} + \ldots + 6 \cdot \frac{1}{6} = 3.5$$

As we can see, the expectation falls in between two of the sample points. This number is the average of the marks on the faces. Now, imagine that someone tampers with the die, making it twice as likely to see a two than any other number. This meddling means that the distribution shifts and that the expectation becomes

$$\mathbb{E}[X] = 1 \cdot \frac{1}{7} + 2 \cdot \frac{2}{7} + 3 \cdot \frac{1}{7} + \ldots + 6 \cdot \frac{1}{7} \approx 3.2857$$

The average under the new distribution is less than under the uniform one. A lower value makes sense since we are more likely to see lower numbers with this die. One thing to note is that this is exactly equivalent to the more familiar way of computing a mean, where we add up some numbers and divide by how many we added. If there are duplicates, that corresponds to a shifted distribution in which that number is more probable.

Variance and Standard Deviation

The expected value is not only useful for computing averages. We could toss any random variable expression into the [·] and compute valid expectations. This notion is exactly what we use to calculate a measurement called *variance*, which we define as

$$\sigma^2 = Var[X] = \mathbb{E}\left[(X - \mu)^2\right]$$

While the notation can look scary at first glance, it has a reasonably straightforward explanation. The variance measures the *spread* of a distribution. That is, it measures the average squared distance between the mean and all sample points.

Squaring the distance makes sure that we add positive values together. If we were to allow negative values, it would come with some strange side effects. For example, the normal distribution (which is symmetrical around the mean) would have zero variance, even though it is evident that there are other sample points besides the one that happens to be the mean.

Since the square can make it more challenging to draw conclusions from the variance, we also have a standard deviation measurement. The standard deviation is nothing more than the square root of the variance, which removes the square from our result while still keeping it nonnegative. Going back to the fair die example, we compute the variance and standard deviation like

$$\sigma^2 = Var[X] = (1-3.5)^2 \cdot \frac{1}{6} + (2-3.5)^2 \cdot \frac{1}{6} + \ldots + (6-3.5)^2 \cdot \frac{1}{6} \approx 2.92$$

$$\sigma = Std[X] = \sqrt{2.92} \approx 1.71$$

These numbers tell us that if we toss a large number of dice, we can expect the spread to be about 1.71 away from the mean value. The variances and standard deviations are used to a great extent when analyzing confidence intervals, and we will put them to use in the coming chapters.

Chapter Summary

This chapter has covered a lot of ground. We have learned how to categorize sample spaces and have seen how that gives rise to two distinct families of distributions – discrete and continuous ones. We have learned how to make calculations using probability mass functions, probability density functions, and cumulative distribution functions. We have also looked at some of the standard distributions used in statistics.

Throughout this book, we will have a lot of use for the theoretical foundation we have built gained until now. The mean, variance, and standard deviation are widely used measurements for describing a distribution, and we will use them in the algorithms we build. Now that we have grasped some of the theoretical concepts we need, we move on to a chapter of more practical application. We will use regression techniques to develop an algorithm that predicts house sale prices based on data.

CHAPTER 4

Predicting House Sale Prices with Linear Regression

So far, we have looked at statistics from the point of describing data. We have tried to find ways of distilling important properties of a potentially massive data set into one or a few numbers. While this approach is undoubtedly practical, we would also like to use the data to look into the future. Thus, we want to look at some sample points that have already happened and use them to predict what happens next. This chapter looks at one way of doing so – this chapter is all about linear regression.

Linear Regression

Linear regression is an idea that, despite its complex name, is surprisingly straightforward. Using previous data points, we want to develop a linear equation that we can use to make decent predictions about new sample points. For example, if we know that one pound of apples costs $1.3, we can compute the price of buying 1.5 pounds. We use the implicit knowledge that not buying anything costs us nothing to create a linear relationship between the weight and the price – we perform a simple form of linear regression. This calculation assumes that a linear equation is

© Jimmy Andersson 2022
J. Andersson, *Statistical Analysis with Swift*, https://doi.org/10.1007/978-1-4842-7765-2_4

appropriately able to describe the relationship between weight and cost. The function we use to predict the total price of apples comes out to

$$price_{apples}(x) = 1.3x, \quad x \in \mathbb{R}_{\geq 0}$$

The kind of linear inter- or extrapolation we saw in the previous example has some benefits. First, it is simple to perform and works very well for many problems. Second, it is also very resource efficient since we don't need to know the price for each individual pound of apples but only need to remember one formula.

However, things become much more complicated when we introduce real-world data. Such sample points are often noisy and do not fit as nicely into this type of tidy mathematical model. For example, take a look at the data set visualized in Figure 4-1.

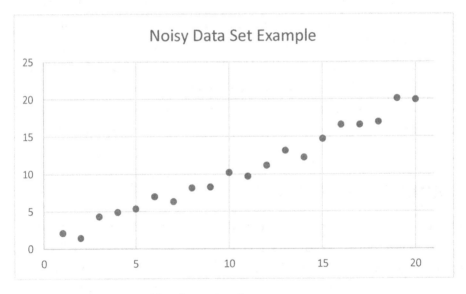

Figure 4-1. *An example of a noisy data set*

The data in Figure 4-1 looks much more like what we would expect from a real-world sample set. The samples come from the following function:

$$f(x) = x + \epsilon, \; \epsilon \sim Normal(0, 1)$$

This formula is a basic linear equation, but it has a variable tagged onto the end. The ϵ is a noise term that adds a random number sampled from a standard normal distribution. This type of added randomness is commonly called Gaussian noise. We can see that the data has a linear tendency, but we cannot connect all points with a single straight line. We need to take another approach to make sense of this data.

Splines

A spline is a mathematical concept that builds on the idea of interpolation. It is different from regression but will act as a stepping stone while developing an intuition for how the technique works and why we need it.

In the case of linear splines, we treat each adjacent pair of points as the endpoints of a range with linear properties, and we connect them with a straight line. Thus, applying it to the previous data set will look like Figure 4-2.

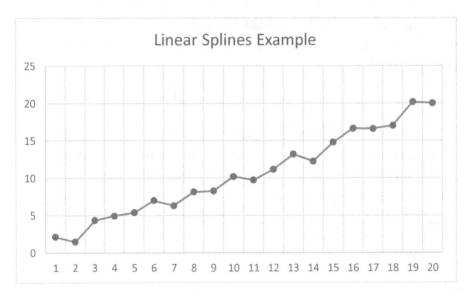

Figure 4-2. *Using linear splines to connect the adjacent sample points by straight line segments*

As we can see, the line is nowhere close to straight when looking at it as a single unit. However, imagine that we want to predict the value for the number 8.4. We would determine that it falls between the original sample points at eight and nine and, consequently, use the linear equation for the spline between those points. In this particular case, that equation is

$$f_{8,9}(x) \approx 8 + 0.113 \cdot (x - 8)$$

$$f_{8,9}(8.4) \approx 8 + 0.113 \cdot (8.4 - 8) \approx 8.045$$

Overall, this approximation is not half bad. However, there are a few scenarios where we run into trouble. A few of them are

- The spline approach forces us to remember parts of the original data to determine which linear equation to use on different intervals. That memory is not a horrible issue if there are few data points, but it quickly becomes unwieldy on data sets that contain millions or billions of entries.

- If we try to make a prediction for a value greater than
  20, we end up using the same linear equation that
  defines values between 19 and 20. Since that equation
  has a negative coefficient in this example, we will
  make smaller predictions farther up the number line.
  Such predictions are a problem since the general
  trend is positive. We can make the same argument
  for predictions on values that are less than one in this
  example.

We conclude that using splines is a reasonable approach on somewhat
small data sets and that they can produce good results as long as they get to
interpolate. However, they are not ideal for larger data sets or when they have
to extrapolate outside of the domain for which they have already seen data.
To improve our methods, we need to address these issues in some way.

Regression Techniques

To make better predictions, we need to address the issues we just lined out.
We want a method with two properties in a situation like this, where we
can see a clear linear tendency in the data.

- It should follow the general trend of the data. A noisy
  measurement should not cause our model to change
  direction and go against that trend, neither inside nor
  outside the range where we have samples.

- We want low computational overhead. Ideally, we
  would like to distill the essential properties of our
  original samples into a few coefficients that can form
  the basis of a linear equation.

Given these properties, our goal is to find the linear equation that best fits the available data. Remember that the general formulation of a straight line is

$$f(x) = kx + m$$

Since x represents the new sample we want to make predictions about, our mission is to determine the variables k and m such that they place $f(x)$ as close to the true value as possible. To do so, we need to define a way of measuring how well we are doing.

Loss Function

The responsibility of a loss function is, as the name implies, to give us an indication of the loss that our current model incurs. A good model should have a low loss value, indicating that it makes predictions that are very close to the measured value of a data point. On the flip side, we want the loss function to return a large number when we make terrible predictions.

One of the main challenges when creating and optimizing models is to design a suitable loss function. The included parameters reflect which pieces of information are important to us. For example, if we want to determine a house's sale price by its square footage, but the loss function only includes the number of rooms, we will never make any good predictions.

Going back to our example data, we want to minimize the collective distance between our predictions and the measured values in the data. For example, if the target value is four, but we predict that it should be three, the distance (or error) is one. By summing over all the errors generated by our model, we can put a number on how well it is doing. We also want to avoid that positive and negative errors cancel out and cause the loss function to become confused. Denoting the number of sample points in our data set by N and the observed value of a sample by y, we can set up the following loss function L that satisfies our needs:

$$\mathcal{L} = \sum_{i=1}^{N}\left(y_i - f(x_i)\right)^2 = \sum_{i=1}^{N}\left(y_i - kx_i - m\right)^2$$

We commonly refer to the previous function as the sum of squares error. The square ensures that the error between a prediction and the target value is always positive. It also maintains the ordering. Thus, if we denote the errors for two points by e_1 and e_2, then

$$e_1 < e_2 \Rightarrow \left(e_1\right)^2 < \left(e_2\right)^2$$

Maintaining this relationship is essential. Introducing a transformation that breaks this ordering could have unintended consequences since good predictions would contribute more to the loss than bad ones.

Now that we have decided on a loss function that satisfies what we want to accomplish, we can start the optimization phase. We consider k and m to be our variables since those are the ones we are interested in optimizing. We begin by computing the Hessian matrix of $\mathcal{L}$ with respect to k and m, which comes out to

$$\boldsymbol{H}_{\mathcal{L}} = \begin{bmatrix} \dfrac{\partial^2 \mathcal{L}}{\partial k^2} & \dfrac{\partial^2 \mathcal{L}}{\partial k\,\partial m} \\[2ex] \dfrac{\partial^2 \mathcal{L}}{\partial m\,\partial k} & \dfrac{\partial^2 \mathcal{L}}{\partial m^2} \end{bmatrix} = \begin{bmatrix} 2\sum_{i=1}^{N}(x_i)^2 & 2\sum_{i=1}^{N}(x_i) \\[2ex] 2\sum_{i=1}^{N}(x_i) & 2N \end{bmatrix}$$

The Hessian is a square matrix of second-order partial derivatives which describes the curvature of a function. We continue to compute the eigenvalues of this matrix and find that

$$\det\left(\boldsymbol{H}_{\mathcal{L}} - \lambda \cdot \boldsymbol{I} \right) = 0$$

$$\lambda^2 - 2\lambda \left(\sum_{i=1}^{N} (x_i)^2 + N \right) = 0$$

$$\lambda = \left(\sum_{i=1}^{N} (x_i)^2 + N \right) \pm \left(\sum_{i=1}^{N} (x_i)^2 + N \right)$$

$$\lambda_1 = 0, \ \lambda_2 = 2(N + \sum_{i=1}^{N} (x^2))$$

While the first eigenvalue is a scalar, we have to analyze the second one a little bit further. We can tell that N will always be positive since we will always have at least one sample point. We also know that any summation over squared values is positive. These realizations lead us to conclude that the second eigenvalue must be positive and that the Hessian matrix is, therefore, positive semi-definite. As we will see next, this has an impact on our ability to find an optimal solution.

Apart from determining the positive semi-definiteness of $\mathbf{H}_L$, we also need to determine whether the domain of our loss function is convex.

A set D is convex if, for any $x_1, x_2 \in D$ and any real valued $\theta \in [0,1]$,
the following holds:

$$\theta x_1 + (1-\theta) x_2 \in D$$

The preceding theorem states that a set is convex if we can pick and combine any two elements and still end up inside the same collection. Figure 4-3 shows a visualization of this concept. No matter which two points we choose inside the circle, the straight line between them only moves through other elements of the same set.

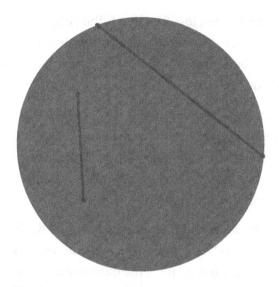

Figure 4-3. *A filled circle is a convex set because the line between any two points moves only through other included points*

The real numbers, ℝ, is a convex set. No matter which two numbers we choose, their convex combination is always another real-valued number. We can conclude that the domain of our problem is convex. With the Hessian matrix being positive semi-definite, this conclusion is a good thing for us. It means that if we can find an optimal solution to our problem, it is guaranteed to be a global optimum.

Finding an Optimal Solution

The last section was hefty on the theory, so let us quickly recap what we have learned and where we want to end up. We have learned that

- We have designed a loss function to help us determine whether our model is making good or bad predictions.

- Since we could establish that the Hessian is positive semi-definite, we can confirm that our loss function is convex on its domain.

- The domain of the loss function is the entire real number line, R. The set of real numbers is convex since it satisfies the conditions in the theorem we saw previously.

- If we can find a local optimum for our loss function (an input value that minimizes the output value), it is guaranteed to be a global optimum. Thanks to this, we do not have to worry about finding any input values that are only locally optimal.

With this knowledge at hand, we are ready to find the linear equation that best fits our observed data. Moreover, now that we know that our problem is convex, we can use one of the oldest optimization tricks in the book – computing the partial derivatives over k and m, setting them to zero, and performing some algebraic gymnastics.

$$\frac{\partial \mathcal{L}}{\partial m} = 0$$

$$-2\sum_{i=1}^{N}(y_i - kx_i - m) = 0$$

$$m = \frac{1}{N}\sum_{i=1}^{N}y_i - k\frac{1}{N}\sum_{i=1}^{N}x_i$$

$$\frac{\partial \mathcal{L}}{\partial k} = 0$$

$$-2\sum_{i=1}^{N}(y_i - kx_i - m)x_i = 0$$

$$k = \frac{N\sum_{i=1}^{N}x_i y_i - \left(\sum_{i=1}^{N}x_i\right)\left(\sum_{i=1}^{N}y_i\right)}{N\sum_{i=1}^{N}(x_i)^2 - \left(\sum_{i=1}^{N}x_i\right)^2}$$

At first glance, these equations may look like we just made things worse. However, we notice something important when we look carefully. The expressions for k and m consist entirely of building blocks from the data set. Thus, all we need to do is perform a few transformations and summations!

Implementing Simple Linear Regression

Now that we have worked out the mathematics of our problem, implementing a solution will be much easier. Let us start by creating a type called `SimpleLinearRegression`. The purpose of this type is to fit a linear equation to some data set. However, we do not want the headache of shaping the data into real number arrays. Instead, we want `SimpleLinearRegression` to take the original data set and retrieve some specified values to use in its calculations. These requirements are a perfect use case for the `KeyPath` type we learned about earlier. Listing 4-1 defines the `struct` and some of its properties.

Listing 4-1. Defining a base type for a simple linear regressor

```
import StatKit

struct SimpleLinearRegression
<Element, X: ConvertibleToReal, Y: ConvertibleToReal>
: CustomStringConvertible {

  let k: Double
  let m: Double

  var description: String {
    let sign = (m.sign == .plus) ? "+" : "-"
    return "\(k)x \(sign) \(abs(m))"
  }
```

```
func predict(x: X) -> Double {
  return k * x.realValue + m
}
}
```

Before moving on to the mathematics, let us quickly walk through the code. There are some fairly advanced concepts at play here, and we need to understand them to make sense of the rest.

- The line that starts with an angle bracket lists some *generic types*. Element is a placeholder for the data we send into the regressor, which can be of any kind. X and Y work as placeholders for the variable types we want to perform our linear regression over. They are constrained such that we are only allowed to use types that conform to the ConvertibleToReal protocol. The protocol comes from StatKit and applies to all types that we can transform into a Double.

- The CustomStringConvertible protocol is part of the Swift standard library and requires us to implement the description property. We use this to tell the system how to describe the regressor when trying to print it.

- The predict(x:) function does what it says. It predicts the value for some input. As we can see, the parameter x is constrained to the generic type X, which is the same constraint we are about to place on the data in the training set.

The only method that is missing is the one that fits the training data. Since a linear regression is tightly coupled to the data we use to fit our function, we can perform the calculations in the initializer. Listing 4-2 defines an initializer for our SimpleLinearRegression.

Listing 4-2. The initializer for `SimpleLinearRegression`

```
init(
  from samples: [Element],
  x: KeyPath<Element, X>,
  y: KeyPath<Element, Y>
) {
  let n = samples.count.realValue

  let (xSum, ySum, xSqSum, xySum) = samples
    .reduce(
      into: (0.0, 0.0, 0.0, 0.0)
    ) { result, point in
      let x = point[keyPath: x].realValue
      let y = point[keyPath: y].realValue
      result.0 += x
      result.1 += y
      result.2 += x * x
      result.3 += x * y
    }

  let kNumerator = (n * xySum - xSum * ySum)
  let kDenominator = (n * xSqSum - xSum * xSum)
  self.k = kNumerator / kDenominator
  self.m = (ySum - k * xSum) / n
}
```

This function is where the mathematical magic happens. As we can see, the generic declarations work to constrain the input values. These constructs give Swift's compiler a chance to help us check the code and provide feedback. We use the KeyPaths we learned about in Chapter 1 to retrieve values for our computations, and we calculate k and m according to the formulas we derived.

These implementations make up the entire SimpleLinearRegression type and are all we need to perform some statistical analysis. Listing 4-3 shows how we can use our new struct to compute the line that best fits our example data.

Listing 4-3. Performing linear regression using our new Swift type

```swift
let points = DataLoader.load(
  Point.self,
  from: .simpleLinearRegression
)
let regressor = SimpleLinearRegression(
  from: points,
  x: \.x,
  y: \.y
)

let x = 5.0
let prediction = regressor.predict(x: x)
let observed = points
  .first(where: { point in
    point.x == 5
  })!.y
print(
  """

  Best fit linear equation for example data
  f(x) = \(regressor)
  Prediction for x = 5
  \(prediction)
  Observed value for x = 5
  \(observed)
  """
)
```

```
// Prints:
// Best fit linear equation for example data
// f(x) = 0.9522649643240606x + 0.4713220140473652
//
// Prediction for x = 5
// 5.232646835667667
//
// Observed value for x = 5
// 5.371954518
```

The amount of glue code needed to perform this regression is minimal, thanks to the linear regression type we just wrote. It is also effortless to reuse if we want to make other regressions. For example, imagine if the data set also contained a z variable. We would only need to create a new regressor and replace the appropriate KeyPath reference with a \.z to make that happen!

Let us take a look at how well this equation describes the data. Figure 4-4 shows the noisy samples we fed into the algorithm and the linear equation we got back.

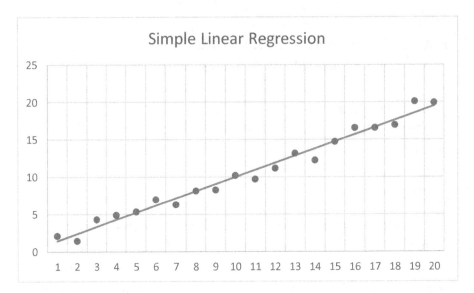

Figure 4-4. *The noisy sample data plotted together with the fitted model from our linear regression*

As we can see, the line describes this data set very well. It follows the general trend, and it is insensitive to local variations. Another plus is that it only requires us to store two floating-point numbers to make any prediction. Furthermore, there is no need to keep the original data around since we already distilled its characteristics. That is very lightweight!

Multiple Linear Regression

We now know how to fit a linear equation to a set of data. This approach requires, quite naturally, that the samples in the data set show some tendency toward a linear relationship. However, most data sets have information about several variables associated with a single data point.

For example, a house sale may not only contain information on the sale price and square footage. There might also be information about the number of rooms, the operating costs, and the year of construction. These are variables that impact the price in one way or another, and it seems reasonable that we should try to take them into account. To develop this idea, we will add another dimension to the example data. Figure 4-5 shows a new data plot with the two feature variables along the X and Y axis and the target variable along the Z axis.

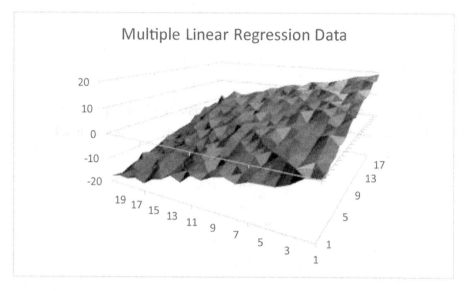

Figure 4-5. *A plot of the expanded example data, which now contains three variables*

As we can see in the plot, the new dimension is also linearly related to the target value. Together, the two feature variables and the target variable form something that reminds us of a slanted and uneven plane. Now that we have a visual intuition of the data, let us get started on the mathematics.

Deriving Linear Regression with Vectors

The mathematical notation we used when developing the simple linear regression is usually fine for one or two variables. However, we may want to use this technique on data with 5, 10, or 50 variables. All of a sudden, the formulas we need to derive have become nightmares. We need a new type of notation to keep the coming equations nice and compact, so we turn to vectors and matrices. Using vector notation, we can denote a sample point and its d features as

$$x = \begin{bmatrix} x_1 \\ x_2 \\ \vdots \\ x_d \\ 1 \end{bmatrix}$$

We append a one to the vector to encompass the intercept, the value that we called m in the single variable case. If we now encapsulate all coefficients and the intercept into a vector **w**, like so

$$w = \begin{bmatrix} w_1 \\ w_2 \\ \vdots \\ w_d \\ w_{d+1} \end{bmatrix}$$

the dot product of these vectors will create an expression that looks like

$$w^T x = w_1 x_1 + w_2 x_2 + \cdots + w_d x_d + w_{d+1} \cdot 1$$

This equation is precisely the predictor we are after. It is a linear expression of every feature variable, plus an intercept variable that we call w_{d+1} in this notation. Like in the simple linear regression case, we want to measure how well this formula captures the training data. We can do that by summing over the squared difference between the observed target value and the prediction, so we can modify the previous loss function to become

$$\mathcal{L} = \sum_{i=1}^{N} \left(y_i - w^T x_i \right)^2 = \sum_{i=1}^{N} \left(y_i - w^T x_i \right)\left(y_i - w^T x_i \right)$$

To further simplify the notation, we can collect all the sample points inside a matrix, which we choose to call **X**. By placing all individual feature vectors as rows in that matrix, we can compute all predictions at once using matrix-vector multiplication. Since that, in turn, produces a vector, we must also stack the target values into a vector format. We call this vector **Y**. The rewritten loss function comes out to

$$\mathcal{L} = (Y - Xw)^{T} (Y - Xw) = Y^{T}Y - 2Y^{T}Xw - w^{T}X^{T}Xw$$

Note that this expression produces a scalar value with the same meaning as in the simple case – it measures the distance between our predictions and the observed values and squares them.

We can try to optimize this expression by performing the same trick as before, the only difference being that we are now computing a gradient. A gradient is a vector of partial derivatives, which conceptually looks like the following:

$$\frac{\partial \mathcal{L}}{\partial w} = \begin{bmatrix} \dfrac{\partial \mathcal{L}}{\partial w_1} \\ \dfrac{\partial \mathcal{L}}{\partial w_2} \\ \vdots \\ \dfrac{\partial \mathcal{L}}{\partial w_d} \\ \dfrac{\partial \mathcal{L}}{\partial w_{d+1}} \end{bmatrix}$$

Calculating the gradient of $\mathcal{L}$ with respect to the vector w, we get

$$\frac{\partial \mathcal{L}}{\partial w} = \frac{\partial}{\partial w} Y^{T}Y - 2Y^{T}Xw - w^{T}X^{T}Xw = 2X^{T}Xw - 2X^{T}Y$$

By setting the gradient equal to the zero vector, we arrive at the following expression:

$$\frac{\partial \mathcal{L}}{\partial w} = 0$$

$$2X^T Xw - 2X^T Y = 0$$

$$X^T Xw = X^T Y$$

To find an optimal solution, we need to realize that X is an n-by-(d+1) matrix. That implies that X^T is a (d+1)-by-n matrix. Such a multiplication produces a square matrix with size (d+1)-by-(d+1).

The *Invertible Matrix Theorem* gives us several conditions for when a square matrix is invertible. One of them, which we will use for our implementation, is that the eigenvalues of our matrix must not include zero. Consequently, if we have a way of telling whether the matrix X^TX only has nonzero eigenvalues, we can perform the following trick by left-multiplying the inverse:

$$\left(X^T X\right)^{-1} X^T Xw = \left(X^T X\right)^{-1} X^T Y$$

$$w = \left(X^T X\right)^{-1} X^T Y$$

This equation gives us an analytical solution to our optimization problem and provides the **w** vector that best fits our data.

Note   Linear regression can also be implemented using the more general Moore-Penrose inverse, which is defined and unique for all matrices with real or complex elements. We will not cover it further in this implementation, but it is an interesting topic and implementation project for those that want to learn more.

Implementing Multiple Linear Regression

Now that we have worked out the mathematics, we are ready to start working on the implementation. In this section, we will introduce the Accelerate framework. Accelerate is a collection of libraries that focus on mathematical calculations and high performance. It uses the CPU's vector processing capabilities to speed up intensive computations and process many values in parallel.

We will reuse the general structure of the `SimpleLinearRegression` struct. We will fit the model in the initializer, use generic types to make the struct reusable across arbitrary data types, target the interesting variables with `KeyPaths`, and use a `predict(x:)` function to make predictions for new data points. However, since we want to target multiple variables, we are going to use variadic parameters. Listing 4-4 shows the new initializer definition we are going to use for this task.

Listing 4-4. The initializer definition for our MultipleLinearRegression type

```
init(from samples: [Element],
     data: KeyPath<Element, X>...,
     target: KeyPath<Element, Y>) throws
```

This initializer looks very much like the one for simple linear regression. The difference lies in the ellipsis appended to the `data` parameter type. This dot-dot-dot syntax makes the argument variadic, meaning that we can target an arbitrary number of variables so long as they fit the declared `KeyPath` type. Listing 4-5 shows two perfectly valid uses of this initializer.

Listing 4-5. Two ways to target different variables using variadic parameters

```
let points: [Point3D] = ...

let singleVar = MultipleLinearRegression(
  from: points,
  data: \.x,
  target: \.z
)

let multiVar = MultipleLinearRegression(
  from: points,
  data: \.x, \.y,
  target: \.z
)
```

As we can see, variadic parameters give us plenty of flexibility when choosing which variables to include in our calculations. This approach makes it easier to perform and test multiple models that target different subsets of our available information.

Now that we have lined out how to use MultipleLinearRegression, let us dig into the details of how it operates. We will split the entire body of the initializer into several listings so that we can reason about each part separately. Starting out, Listing 4-6 shows the initial setup.

Listing 4-6. The initial setup performed by the MultipleLinearRegression initializer

```
let sampleCount = Int32(samples.count)
let dimCount32 = Int32(data.count + 1)
let dimCount64 = data.count + 1
let XTransXDimension = dimCount64 * dimCount64
```

```
var X = samples.flatMap { sample -> [Double] in
  var row = data.map { keyPath in
    sample[keyPath: keyPath].realValue
  }

  row.append(1)
  return row
}

var XTrans = X

var Y = samples.map { sample in
  return sample[keyPath: target].realValue
}

var XTransX = [Double](
  repeating: 0,
  count: XTransXDimension
)
var XTransY = [Double](
  repeating: 0,
  count: dimCount64
)
```

The first thing we do is to set up some of the data structures we need. We create count variables for the number of samples and the data dimensions. Note that the variables dimCount32 and dimCount64 are the same value, only differing by their type. One could choose to use a single variable and typecast it when needed, but this will reduce the cognitive noise from reading such code.

We create our **X** matrix by using flatMap(_:), which is a higher-order function just like map(_:) and filter(_:). It works similar to map(_:), but expects us to create a sequence of values for each data point. It then takes all arrays we make and merge them into one, with the *k* elements from the first data point taking the first k indices in the sequence. One consequence of this approach is that we have a one-dimensional representation of a two-dimensional data structure. Instead of keeping nested arrays, as you would in many other languages, we lay out each row sequentially after each other. This layout is called row-major order. The opposite would be to place each matrix column after each other, aptly named column-major order.

XTrans is the matrix we call $\mathbf{X}^T$ in our mathematical notation. It is easy to see that it is not the transpose of $\mathbf{X}$ but just a plain copy. However, that is okay since the function calls we will use from the Accelerate framework offer to compute a matrix's transpose before performing their main calculations.

Y is the vector that contains the target values, that is, the observed value for each sample point. Since we want to minimize the number of mathematical operations we need to perform before reaching a result, we prefer matrix-vector multiplication before matrix-matrix multiplication. However, we cannot escape computing $(\mathbf{X}^T\mathbf{X})^{-1}$ separately. To minimize the work, we will split our calculations into three steps:

$$Step\ 1: Compute\ \boldsymbol{M} = \left(\boldsymbol{X}^T\boldsymbol{X}\right)^{-1} \quad \left(matrix - matrix\right)$$

$$Step\ 2: Compute\ \boldsymbol{V} = \boldsymbol{X}^T\boldsymbol{Y} \quad \left(matrix - vector\right)$$

$$Step\ 3: Compute\ \boldsymbol{R} = \boldsymbol{MV} \quad \left(matrix - vector\right)$$

Because we want to take this approach, we also set up the arrays **XTransX** and **XTransY**. Note that we have declared all arrays with the var keyword. We do so because we need to pass pointers to the Accelerate methods. Because pointers can mutate the underlying storage, we need the variables to be mutable.

Now that we have allocated some of the storage we need for our calculations, let us go ahead and make our first calls to the Accelerate framework. We will start by using the method shown in Listing 4-7.

Listing 4-7. One of the many matrix-vector multiplication methods that are available through the Accelerate framework

```
func cblas_dgemv(
    _ __Order: CBLAS_ORDER,
    _ __TransA: CBLAS_TRANSPOSE,
    _ __M: Int32,
    _ __N: Int32,
    _ __alpha: Double,
    _ __A: UnsafePointer<Double>!,
    _ __lda: Int32,
    _ __X: UnsafePointer<Double>!,
    _ __incX: Int32,
    _ __beta: Double,
    _ __Y: UnsafeMutablePointer<Double>!,
    _ __incY: Int32
)
```

Those that have a little bit of experience with Swift development will notice that this declaration looks different than most other Swift code they have seen. That is because this (and some of the other functions we will use) refers to Apple's implementation of the *Basic Linear Algebra Subprograms* for C (CBLAS). Swift has the convenient capability to be able to import C functions. This feature is handy but comes with the minor inconvenience that the code looks less modern when using these interfaces.

Going back to the function in Listing 4-7, we quickly go through what it expects us to pass to the different parameters:

- **__Order**: This parameter specifies the order of the matrix we want to use for multiplication. Since we chose to structure our matrices in row-major order, we pass CblasRowMajor as an argument.

- **__TransA**: Whether the function should transpose our matrix before performing multiplication. We did not precompute the transpose, so we pass `CblasTrans`.

- **__M**: The number of rows in the original matrix. Since we place our sample points on each row, we have `sampleCount` rows.

- **__N**: The number of columns in the original matrix. Our matrix will have `dimCount32` columns.

- **__alpha**: This parameter scales the result of our multiplication by some amount. We want an unaltered scale, so we pass in 1.

- **__A**: A pointer to our matrix.

- **__lda**: The leading dimension of our matrix. Since we chose row-major order, we will pass in the number of columns, which is `dimCount32`.

- **__X**: A pointer to our vector.

- **__incX**: The stride to use when moving through the vector **__X**.

- **__Y**: A pointer to a structure that can store the resulting vector.

- **__incY**: The stride to use when moving through **__Y**.

The BLAS interfaces are certainly a lot to take in. Listing 4-8 shows one more BLAS function declaration, which we will use for matrix-matrix multiplication. However, we will not explain those arguments since they are very similar to those in the function from Listing 4-7.

Listing 4-8. One of multiple available BLAS functions for matrix-matrix multiplication

```
func cblas_dgemm(
    _ __Order: CBLAS_ORDER,
    _ __TransA: CBLAS_TRANSPOSE,
    _ __TransB: CBLAS_TRANSPOSE,
    _ __M: Int32,
    _ __N: Int32,
    _ __K: Int32,
    _ __alpha: Double,
    _ __A: UnsafePointer<Double>!,
    _ __lda: Int32,
    _ __B: UnsafePointer<Double>!,
    _ __ldb: Int32,
    _ __beta: Double,
    _ __C: UnsafeMutablePointer<Double>!,
    _ __ldc: Int32
)
```

Note   We are only scratching the surface of all you can do with the BLAS interfaces. To dive deeper, feel free to visit IBM's documentation for the *Engineering and Scientific Subroutine Library*, which features well-documented implementations of BLAS routines.

www.ibm.com/docs/en/essl

Now that we know how to use the matrix and vector multiplication methods, we can add the code listed in Listing 4-9 to our initializer.

Listing 4-9. Computing X^TX and X^TY for our multiple linear regression

```
cblas_dgemv(
  CblasRowMajor,
  CblasTrans,
  sampleCount,
  dimCount32,
  1,
  &XTrans,
  dimCount32,
  &Y,
  1,
  1,
  &XTransY,
  1
)

cblas_dgemm(
  CblasRowMajor,
  CblasTrans,
  CblasNoTrans,
  dimCount32,
  dimCount32,
  sampleCount,
  1,
  &XTrans,
  dimCount32,
  &X,
  dimCount32,
```

```
1,
&XTransX,
dimCount32
)
```

Before we can perform our last matrix-vector multiplication and get a result, we need to invert $\mathbf{X^TX}$. To do so, we will use a set of LAPACK routines, namely, dgetrf_ and dgetri_. These two functions work together to perform an LU factorization of a matrix and later solving a system of equations to find the inverse of the same. Listing 4-10 shows the declarations of these functions.

Listing 4-10. Declarations of the LAPACK functions dgetrf_ and dgetri_

```
func dgetrf_(
  _ __m: UnsafeMutablePointer<__CLPK_integer>!,
  _ __n: UnsafeMutablePointer<__CLPK_integer>!,
  _ __a: UnsafeMutablePointer<__CLPK_doublereal>!,
  _ __lda: UnsafeMutablePointer<__CLPK_integer>!,
  _ __ipiv: UnsafeMutablePointer<__CLPK_integer>!,
  _ __info: UnsafeMutablePointer<__CLPK_integer>!
) -> Int32

func dgetri_(
  _ __n: UnsafeMutablePointer<__CLPK_integer>!,
  _ __a: UnsafeMutablePointer<__CLPK_doublereal>!,
  _ __lda: UnsafeMutablePointer<__CLPK_integer>!,
  _ __ipiv: UnsafeMutablePointer<__CLPK_integer>!,
  _ __work: UnsafeMutablePointer<__CLPK_doublereal>!,
  _ __lwork: UnsafeMutablePointer<__CLPK_integer>!,
  _ __info: UnsafeMutablePointer<__CLPK_integer>!
) -> Int32
```

Granted, if the BLAS methods looked a little bit scary, then these look like proper nightmares. However, once we figure out a little bit more about what goes on behind the curtains, even these methods will be helpful.

__CLPK_integer and __CLPK_doublereal are just type aliases for Int32 and Double. Just knowing that already makes the cognitive strain go away a little bit. The parameters __m and __n are matrix dimensions, just like they were in the other functions. Parameter __a represents the matrix we want to invert, and __lda is the leading dimension just like before. __ipiv represents a collection of pivot indices used to tell how the functions rearrange the rows during the factorization process. __work and __lwork are a workspace array and its dimension, respectively. According to IBM's documentation, the workspace's size should be at least a hundred times the size of __n for the algorithm to achieve good performance. Finally, the __info parameter returns information about failures to the developer. For one, it tells us whether the matrix we are trying to invert has eigenvalues that include zero. This mechanism is the fail-safe we talked about back in the discussion on the *Invertible Matrix Theorem*.

To use these functions, we need to set up a few more arrays and supporting variables. We also need to declare an error enum we can use to propagate any failures. Listing 4-11 shows the enum, while Listing 4-12 lists the setup, together with the calls to dgetrf_ and dgetri_.

Listing 4-11. The definition of the error struct we use to propagate errors

```
enum LinearRegressionError: Error {
  case singularMatrix
  case invalidArguments
}
```

Listing 4-12. Setting up a workspace and computing $(X^TX)^{-1}$

```
var m = dimCount32
var n = dimCount32
var lda = dimCount32
var workspaceSize = 100 * m

var pivots = [Int32](
  repeating: 0,
  count: dimCount64
)
var workspace = [Double](
  repeating: 0,
  count: Int(workspaceSize)
)
var luError = Int32.zero
var invError = Int32.zero
dgetrf_(&m, &n, &XTransX, &lda, &pivots, &luError)

switch luError {
  case ..<0:
    throw LinearRegressionError.invalidArguments
  case 1...:
    throw LinearRegressionError.singularMatrix
  default:
    break
}

dgetri_(&m, &XTransX, &lda, &pivots, &workspace,
&workspaceSize, &invError)

switch invError {
  case ..<0:
    throw LinearRegressionError.invalidArguments
```

```
case 1...:
  throw LinearRegressionError.singularMatrix
default:
  break
}
```

Once these calls return, the inverted matrix $(\mathbf{X}^T\mathbf{X})^{-1}$ resides in the variable called XTransX. Assuming that dgetrf_ and dgetri_ exited cleanly, and we did not throw any errors, we now have the two components we need to compute the vector **w** – the dimCount32 by dimCount32 matrix $(\mathbf{X}^T\mathbf{X})^{-1}$ and the dimCount32-length vector $\mathbf{X}^T\mathbf{Y}$. All that remains is to perform one more matrix-vector multiplication to get our final result. Listing 4-13 shows the final stretch of code in our initializer, featuring our friend cblas_dgemv(_:_:_:_:_:_:_:_:_:_:_:_:).

Listing 4-13. The final stretch of our code for our initializer method

```
var w = [Double](repeating: 0, count: dimCount64)

cblas_dgemv(
  CblasRowMajor,
  CblasTrans,
  dimCount32,
  dimCount32,
  1,
  &XTransX,
  dimCount32,
  &XTransY,
  1,
  1,
  &w,
  1
)
```

```
self.w = w
self.variables = data
```

Finishing up the calculations in the initializer, we create some storage for w, perform the final multiplication, and then store the computed coefficients and the KeyPaths in the data parameter for later use.

We finished the implementation of the learning algorithm, which is a significant milestone in itself. However, it does not have any real value if we cannot use it to make predictions, so we also need to implement the predict(x:) function. To do so, we will use one more BLAS routine. Remember that we defined our predictions as

$$\boldsymbol{w}^T \boldsymbol{x} = w_1 x_1 + w_2 x_2 + \ldots + w_d x_d + w_{d+1} \cdot 1$$

We already have easy access to $\boldsymbol{w}^T$ thanks to the initializer we just implemented. However, we need to create a new feature vector for the sample point we want to predict. Fortunately, we have a procedure to do that since we already made a whole set of feature vectors for our matrix $\mathbf{X}$. That leaves us with the task of performing the summation. We could use a higher-order function like reduce(_:) to multiply and sum all of the elements. This approach is completely acceptable for small feature sets or when making predictions for a limited number of data points. However, it might take a long time if either the feature set or the number of data points is large. Let us explore a way of making this calculation with the help of BLAS. Listing 4-14 shows the declaration of a function that computes the dot product of two vectors.

Listing 4-14. One of the multiple BLAS routines that computes dot products

```
func cblas_ddot(
  _ __N: Int32,
  _ __X: UnsafePointer<Double>!,
  _ __incX: Int32,
```

```
    _ _Y: UnsafePointer<Double>!,
    _ _incY: Int32
) -> Double
```

The parameters of this function have similar meanings to the ones of the matrix-vector and matrix-matrix multiplication methods, but let us quickly walk through them:

- __N: This parameter specifies the number of elements from each vector to include in the dot product. It can be at most as great as the length of the smallest vector, or weird things will happen. For our linear regression, it will be the same length as **w**.

- __X: This parameter takes a pointer to the first vector. In our case, this is **w**.

- __incX: The stride of vector __X. Since we want all of the elements in our sum, we set this to 1.

- __Y: A pointer to the second vector. We will pass one that refers to the feature vector of a data point.

- __incY: Just like __incX, this specifies the stride inside vector __Y. We will set this to 1 as well.

Now that we have covered the different parts that go into the prediction, let us implement the final piece of `MultipleLinearRegression`. The code in Listing 4-15 shows the function.

Listing 4-15. The final function before we can make use of our work with a multiple linear regression type

```
func predict(x: Element) -> Double {
  var features = variables.map { keyPath in
    x[keyPath: keyPath].realValue
  }
```

```
features.append(1)
let n = Int32(w.count)
var w = w

return cblas_ddot(
  n,
  &w,
  1,
  &features,
  1
)
}
```

As we can see, the mapping of features is very similar to the one we performed when we learned the linear function in our initializer. The only difference is that we only create a single feature vector instead of putting multiple rows into a matrix construct. Overall, this function is very concise and does not take too much effort to read and grasp.

All this work has led to a functioning algorithm for learning a linear regression and making predictions. Listing 4-16 contains some code from the accompanying code project, which shows how we can use our new Swift type on an example data set. Remember that we need to wrap our use in a do-catch clause to handle any thrown errors. There is also a new implementation of the description property to print our new linear equation. It is, however, left out of this listing for brevity.

Listing 4-16. An example of how to use our new MultipleLinearRegression type

```
let points = DataLoader.load(
  Point3D.self,
  from: .multipleLinearRegression
)
```

```
do {
  let regressor = try MultipleLinearRegression(
    from: points,
    data: \.x, \.y,
    target: \.z
  )

  let observed = points[42]
  let prediction = regressor.predict(x: observed)

  print(
    """

    f(x) = \(regressor)
    Prediction for (\(observed.x), \(observed.y))
    \(prediction)
    Observed value for (\(observed.x), \(observed.y))
    \(observed.z)
    """

  )
}
catch {
  print("An error was thrown: \(error)")
}

// Prints:
// f(x) = 1.010083366089924 * x_1 -
// 0.9873800441120847 * x_2 - 0.23672317614604843
// Prediction for (3.0, 3.0)
// -0.16861321021253062
// Observed value for (3.0, 3.0)
// -0.379395117657068
```

Predicting House Sale Prices

After finishing the development of new tools, it is always fun to try them out on fun data sets. The code project contains a file called HousePricePredictions.swift that we can use for precisely that purpose. It loads a data set containing generated house sale data, which follows a similar distribution to 12,500 recent sales made in four large cities in Sweden. Feel free to explore the data and play around with which variables give you the smallest loss value. Think about the nature of the different variables, whether they are naturally representable by real or integer numbers, and how that affects the regression.

Chapter Summary

In this chapter, we covered quite a bit of theory from both the mathematical and engineering side. We learned about simple linear extrapolation between two data points and how it breaks when our samples become too irregular. We also made a stop at linear splines and discussed how and why they can be helpful and why they are not well suited for large data sets. These discussions later landed us in the territory of linear regression by helping us understand the shortcomings it addresses.

In the sections on linear regression, we learned about loss functions, which help us determine how well a particular model describes our observed data. We also derived the theory around linear regression with the help of said loss function and made two implementations – one for the simple case and one for multivariate ones. The latter took us through BLAS and LAPACK and showed us some of the tools at our disposal when solving these problems.

Modeling the real world is a beneficial skill when trying to make predictions about it. However, it is an equally handy skill to look at two sets of observed data and assess whether some important metrics have changed significantly. This problem set is what we will look at in the next chapter.

CHAPTER 5

Hypothesis Testing

Hypothesis testing is a valuable area of statistics. It can aid us when working with random variables that may change their distributions over time or because of certain events. However, it is also one of the topics that students find most daunting and challenging to understand. In this chapter, we look at several examples of formulating a hypothesis and leveraging Swift to determine whether it is more likely than the currently accepted truth.

What Is Hypothesis Testing?

To get a feeling for why hypothesis testing is helpful, let us look at an example statement:

> The dean of a university claims that the attending students have above-average intelligence. Thirty randomly sampled students agree to take an IQ test, on which they score an average of 105 according to the Wechsler Adult Intelligence Scale (WAIS). Is the dean's claim correct?

While this particular example may not be part of the everyday tasks of a data scientist or statistician, it will help us reason about a few questions that we need to consider.

© Jimmy Andersson 2022
J. Andersson, *Statistical Analysis with Swift*, https://doi.org/10.1007/978-1-4842-7765-2_5

WAIS is normally distributed, with an average score of 100 and a standard deviation of 15. Since the students scored an average of 105, which is greater than the WAIS average of 100, it may be tempting to conclude that the dean is correct. However, some questions arise from this way of reasoning.

- Even if the scores differ, they only do so by 5%. Is that enough of a difference to make such a general claim?

- What if we got lucky when we chose the students that took the test? Maybe the students that participated scored higher than the rest of the students would.

- How do we measure the uncertainty that comes from the previous questions? Can we produce a number that tells us how confident we can be in our results?

As we can see, there are many things we need to take into account before we can tell whether the claims in this example make any sense or if we should reject them. First, we need to establish terminology that makes it easier to use mathematical tools to solve the problems.

Formulating Hypotheses

To solve these problems, we first need to formalize the hypotheses we want to test. Beginners often struggle with this part, and the main reason seems to be because it is not always easy to pick out relevant information about a problem. To get comfortable formulating hypotheses, we will describe the two different kinds of hypotheses we need to formulate for any problem and show a few examples to get comfortable with the ideas. Right now, we will focus on the high-level concepts, and more details will follow in the later sections.

The Null Hypothesis

The null hypothesis, denoted by H_0, describes a commonly accepted fact. It suggests that there is no significant difference between the samples we collect and the currently accepted ground truth. For example, a car manufacturer might specify that a particular model gets an average of 23 miles per gallon. The null hypothesis then suggests that any data we collect by testing some cars of the same model will yield an average of 23 miles per gallon. The mathematical formulation of this hypothesis comes out to

$$H_0: \quad \mu = 23\,mpg$$

That is it! Nothing more, nothing less. We state that, according to H_0, the average μ is equal to 23 miles per gallon.

The Alternative Hypothesis

The alternative hypothesis, which we denote by H_A, is a claim that we want to investigate. It suggests a new scenario in which the null hypothesis no longer holds. For example, the car manufacturer from the previous example may recently have made changes to the production line. Because of those changes, we believe that the new cars no longer get 23 miles per gallon. However, we do not have an opinion on whether the changes improved or worsened the gas mileage. It may be higher or lower than before. In mathematical notation, we denote this hypothesis by

$$H_A: \quad \mu \neq 23\,mpg$$

The alternative hypothesis looks just as simple as the null hypothesis from the previous section. One important thing to note is that the null and alternative hypotheses are each other's complements. That is, they cover every possible outcome. In this example, the average gas mileage is either

23 mpg or something else. There is no possible way to construct a scenario in which both hypotheses are true or false at the same time.

The fact that the null and alternative hypotheses are each other's complements allows us to dive deeper and explore other questions. Can we use other complementary relations to be more flexible in how and what we test?

Tails

The way we formulated our alternative hypothesis in the previous section was not technically incorrect. However, it did feel odd to hypothesize that the average gas mileage had changed while not indicating the direction. There are certainly times when all we need is to test whether a statistic has moved in either direction, but there are also times when we want to be more specific.

Imagine that the changes made to the production line in the previous example mean that the combustion chambers now come from a partner with better technologies available, making the parts much more high quality. With such additional knowledge, we may feel comfortable hypothesizing that the average gas mileage has increased. Making that assumption means that the H_0 and H_A we formulated before no longer describe our hypotheses. Instead, our alternative hypothesis says that the average is greater than 23 mpg. Because H_0 and H_A need to be complements of each other, the null hypothesis must be that the average is less than or equal to 23. Mathematically, our new hypotheses look like the following:

$$H_0: \quad \mu \leq 23\,mpg$$

$$H_A: \quad \mu > 23\,mpg$$

While this does not precisely capture the currently accepted average gas mileage, this formulation does have some nice properties. Firstly, it allows us to encapsulate additional information into the alternative hypothesis by specifying in which direction we believe the average has changed. Secondly, even though the null hypothesis extends from 23 miles per gallon and downward, it still contains the car manufacturer's original claim.

We call this new formulation a *one-tailed test* simply because it specifies a single direction in which we believe the statistic has changed. The same term would apply if we instead believed that the average had shifted downward. The first example only hypothesized that the average had changed. However, it did not specify a direction and is therefore called a *two-tailed test*.

We can further subdivide one-tailed tests into *left-tailed* and *right-tailed* tests. This categorization depends on the exact direction of the believed change. We use a left-tailed test for when H_A specifies a decrease in the statistic, while a right-tailed test specifies an increase.

One crucial thing to note is that hypothesis testing says nothing about whether the hypotheses are true. It only says something about which one is more likely, given the data we collected. It might sound strange, but the explanation is pretty straightforward. Just because we might end up showing that one option is more likely than the other does not necessarily mean that it is true. Proving that a hypothesis or theory is true is a much more difficult task.

Now that we have defined some terminology around hypothesis testing, it is time to dive deeper into the details. First of all, one-tailed and two-tailed tests are somewhat simple to understand, given how we have defined them so far. However, we have yet to uncover what these "tails" are. To get a grip on that, we need to ask ourselves a few questions about the distribution of sample means.

Distribution of Sample Means

Imagine that there are 100 folded notes in a hat. On each note is a number between zero and five. Our task is to compute the average of those numbers, but we can only look at 30 randomly selected notes. This scenario has a few different possible outcomes.

- We could end up selecting the notes with the highest numbers on them. In that case, our result could be much greater than the true mean. However, the odds of selecting exactly those notes are relatively small.

- Similarly, we could end up selecting all the smallest numbers. In this case, our computation of the mean would be too small compared to the true one. The probability of hitting this scenario is also relatively small.

- The most likely outcomes lie somewhere in between the two extremes described earlier. We will probably select some mix of larger and smaller numbers, and taking the average of those will yield a result that is at least somewhat close to the true mean.

This type of distribution may already start to sound a bit familiar from Chapter 3. Let us write some code to visualize the distribution of sample means from some set. Listing 5-1 shows the initializer of a SwiftUI View that receives an array of numbers, which it uses to compute a large number of sample means. We then visualize these results by plotting them in a histogram inside the body property, as shown in Listing 5-2.

Listing 5-1. Computing and plotting multiple sample means

```
init(
  numberOfMeans: Int,
  numberOfSamples: Int,
  sampledFrom set: [Double]
) {
  precondition(
    !set.isEmpty,
    "Samples need to contain at least one element."
  )
  // Used to place values into a histogram bin
  let rounding = 0.1

  let meansIterator = (1 ... numberOfMeans).lazy
  let samplesIterator = (1 ... numberOfSamples).lazy

  self.data = meansIterator
    .map { _ in
      samplesIterator
        .compactMap { _ in set.randomElement() }
        .mean(of: \.self)
    }
    .reduce(into: [Double: Int]()) { dict, mean in
      let roundedMean = (mean / rounding)
        .rounded() * rounding
      dict[roundedMean, default: 0] += 1
    }
    .map { key, value in
      BarChartDataEntry(
        x: key,
        y: value.realValue / numberOfMeans.realValue
      )
    }
```

```
  self.barWidth = 0.9 * rounding
  self.mean = set.mean(of: \.self)
  self.numberOfSamples = numberOfSamples
}
```

Listing 5-2. Displaying the computed sample means in a histogram

```
var body: some View {
  VStack(spacing: 20) {
    Text("Computing Sample Means")
      .font(.largeTitle)

    HStack(spacing: 20) {
      Text("True mean: \(mean, specifier: "%.3f")")
      Text("Samples per mean: \(numberOfSamples)")
    }
    .padding(.horizontal)

    Histogram(
      data: data,
      label: "Distribution of sample means",
      barWidth: barWidth,
      xAxisMin: 0,
      xAxisMax: 5
    )
  }
}
```

Running the code listed previously on a set of 100 uniform random numbers between zero and five produces a histogram like the one in Figure 5-1. The code computed a total of 5,000 sample means, using a sample size of 30 for each mean.

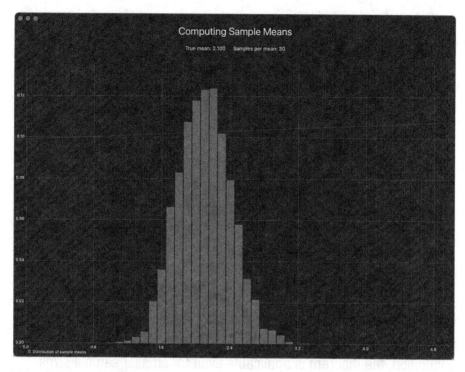

Figure 5-1. *Computing 5,000 sample means from a set of 100 uniform random numbers*

Looking at this histogram, we have a visualization that supports the suspicion that came about when we listed the different outcomes of computing sample means. The columns form a shape that looks very much like a normal distribution! This result is not a coincidence but is formalized in a theorem that data scientists and statisticians use regularly.

The Central Limit Theorem

The Central Limit Theorem makes life a whole lot easier for anyone who wants to perform hypothesis testing. It tells us that the distribution of sample means from a population can be approximated by a normal distribution. This result holds regardless of whether the distribution we

117

sample from is normal. However, there are a few conditions we need to fulfill.

- We need to sample with replacement. For example, once we have chosen one student to perform an IQ test, we cannot remove them from the sample pool since that would alter the distribution for the remaining samples. Instead, we need to be okay with the possibility of choosing the same student multiple times.

- We need the sample size to be sufficiently large. That is, we cannot randomly select two or three students. One commonly accepted limit is that we need at least 30 samples for this theorem to be applicable.

Note   There is one exception to the sample size limit mentioned previously. If the samples come from a normally distributed population, the theorem is applicable even for smaller sample sizes than 30.

Given that the preceding conditions hold, the Central Limit Theorem tells us that we can approximate the distribution of a sample mean by a normal distribution. When we discussed the normal distribution in Chapter 3, we mentioned that the mean μ and standard deviation σ define the exact shape of the characteristic bell curve. We estimate those parameters by the following formulas:

$$\mu_{est} = \frac{1}{N} \sum_{i=1}^{N} \overline{x}_i$$

$$\sigma_{est} = S = \frac{1}{N-1} \sum_{i=1}^{N} \left(\overline{x}_i - \mu \right)^2$$

In these formulas, we denote an individual sample mean by an x with a bar on top. We denote the sample standard deviation by an S. These are both unbiased estimators of the true mean and standard deviation, making them acceptable substitutes when we do not know the actual values. In those cases where we already know the mean and standard deviation of the population, we can instead use the following:

$$\mu_{est} = \mu_{population}$$

$$\sigma_{est} = \frac{\sigma_{population}}{\sqrt{N}}$$

N denotes the sample size in these equations and is used to scale the population's standard deviation. The derivation and proof of the previous formulas are beyond the scope of this book. However, we will look at two examples to get a visual indication that they hold.

Figure 5-2 shows a gamma distribution with parameters $\alpha = 3$ and $\beta = 3$. Figure 5-3 shows a density histogram of 1000 sample means of sample size 30. It also shows an overlaid normal distribution curve with parameters estimated according to the formulas that estimate an unknown mean and standard deviation.

Figure 5-4 shows a more interesting distribution. It is a linear combination of two beta distributions, one with parameters $\alpha = 7$ and $\beta = 2$ and the other one with $\alpha = 2$ and $\beta = 5$. Figure 5-5 shows a histogram of sample means and a normal distribution curve with appropriate, estimated parameters.

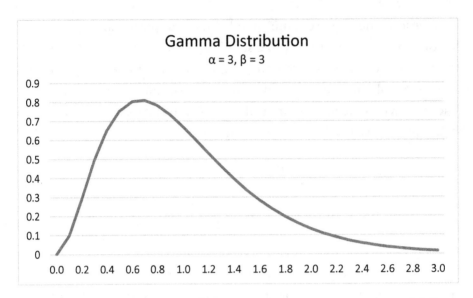

Figure 5-2. *A gamma distribution with parameters α = 3 and β = 3*

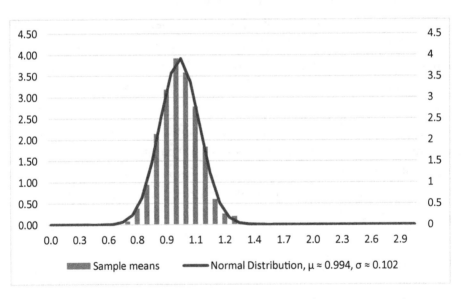

Figure 5-3. *The distribution of 1000 sample means computed from the gamma distribution in Figure 5-2 and an overlaid normal distribution with parameters μ ≈ 0.994 and σ ≈ 0.102*

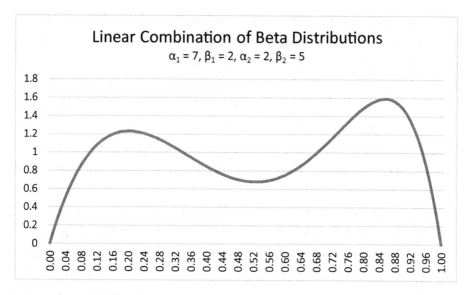

Figure 5-4. *A distribution made up of a linear combination of two beta distributions*

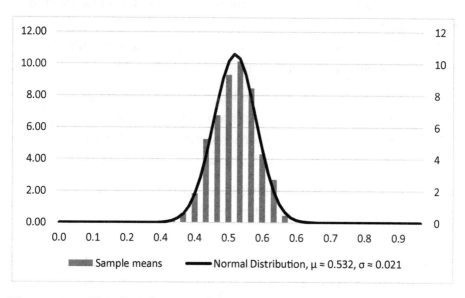

Figure 5-5. *The distribution of 1000 sample means computed from the linear combination of beta distributions in Figure 5-4 and an overlaid normal distribution with parameters $\mu \approx 0.532$ and $\sigma \approx 0.021$*

Let us first discuss the gamma distribution. Plotting all 1000 sample means in a histogram shows us that the distribution is bell shaped. When we compare it to a normal distribution with our estimated parameters μ and σ, we can see that they match very well. We can also note that the estimated mean, μ, is very close to the true mean of this distribution, which is 1. One could perhaps argue that this particular gamma distribution looks a little bit like a skewed normal distribution and that the approximation, therefore, becomes better. However, looking at the subsequent figures, we can see that is not the case.

The linear combination of two beta distributions forms an interesting shape. It has two peaks and looks nothing like a normal distribution. Still, computing 1000 sample means with a sample size of 30 and plotting them in a histogram shows a distribution that has a very similar shape to the one in the gamma example. Comparing it to the curve of a normal distribution, we see that even though they do not fit quite as well as in the first example, the match is still impressive given how odd looking the original distribution is.

Now that we know that a normal distribution can approximate the distribution of sample means, we can address what a tail is:

- A left-tailed test is interested in how small the sample mean needs to be before it is considered a statistical anomaly. That is, how much lower than μ does it have to be before it is too small to have come up by chance?

- A right-tailed test describes the opposite: how large a sample mean must be before it is too large to be a coincidence.

- A two-tailed test is interested in how much the sample mean must differ from μ in any direction before we are comfortable saying that it cannot be by random chance.

With this theory covered, we are ready to determine what we consider "too unlikely" and start testing some hypotheses!

Testing the Hypothesis

The tools and theory we have gone through are just about all that we need to tell whether the university's dean is correct in their claim. Let us start by formulating our null and alternative hypotheses. In this case, we are investigating a claim that the dean's students have above-average intelligence. The null hypothesis must be the complement, which is that they have equal to or below-average intelligence. The mean intelligence score according to WAIS is 100, which gives us

$$H_0: \quad \mu \leq 100$$

$$H_A: \quad \mu > 100$$

The next step in the process is to decide how confident we want to be in our decision. Suppose we decide that the university students have, in fact, above-average intelligence. In that case, we want to minimize the chance that all the students we sampled come from the top IQ segment on campus. We want to determine a confidence level and an alpha value.

Determining Confidence Levels

A confidence level, commonly denoted by the letter c, determines how certain we need to be of our results to reject the null hypothesis. It tells us how much the test statistic must differ from μ before the alternative hypothesis becomes more likely than the null hypothesis. If we decide that we want to be 95% certain, then

$$c = 0.95$$

Besides telling us where to draw the line between rejecting and keeping the null hypothesis, the confidence level also plays a part in justifying our decisions when explaining it to others. If we end up rejecting the null hypothesis, thereby saying that the university's students are brighter than average, a confidence level of 0.95 would mean that we are at least 95% certain that the decision is correct.

Determining Alpha Values

On the opposite side of the confidence level is the alpha value, denoted by the Greek letter α. We define it as

$$\alpha = 1 - c$$

If we wanted a confidence level of 0.95, then α would be 0.05. While the confidence level specifies how sure we want to be of the results, the alpha acts from the opposite end. In this case, it says that there can only be a 5% chance that the distribution from H_0 produces a sample mean that is more extreme than the one we calculate.

Performing the Test

Let us decide on a confidence level of 0.95, which consequently means an alpha value of 0.05. The sampled students have produced an average score of 105. WAIS is normally distributed, with $\mu = 100$ and $\sigma = 15$. We want to know how likely it is that the WAIS distribution produces a sample mean that is greater than 105 – that is:

$$P[x > 105] = 1 - P[x < 105]$$

If it is less than 5%, then we can confidently reject the null hypothesis and confirm that the dean's claim is probably correct. The code in Listing 5-3 shows a small Swift program that computes and prints the information we want.

Listing 5-3. A Swift script that tests the dean's hypothesis

```swift
let numberOfStudents = 30.0
let WAISAverage = 100.0
let WAISSD = 15.0
let computedAverageScore = 105.0
let sdScalar = sqrt(numberOfStudents.realValue)

let normalDist = NormalDistribution(
  mean: WAISAverage,
  standardDeviation: WAISSD / sdScalar
)

let probability = 1 - normalDist.cdf(x: computedAverageScore)
let confidence = 1 - probability
let probString = String(
  format: "%.2f",
  probability * 100
)
let confString = String(
  format: "%.2f",
  confidence * 100
)
print(
  """

  There is a \(probString)% chance that the computed
  average belongs to the null hypothesis.
  We can be \(confString)% confident if we reject
  the null hypothesis!
  """

)
```

```
// Prints:
// There is a 3.39% chance that the computed
// average belongs to the null hypothesis.
// We can be 96.61% confident if we reject
// the null hypothesis!
```

As we can see, scoring an average of 105 on the WAIS test was not as likely as one perhaps could have thought. There is only a 3.4% chance that we are wrong if we choose to reject the null hypothesis – consequently meaning that we can be about 96.6% certain that we are correct. Since we wanted to be at least 95% sure, we can tell the dean that they have every reason to be proud of the students.

Chapter 5 in the code project contains a SwiftUI View called `IQHypothesisTest.swift`, which computes and displays this result depending on which values we put into the different fields. Feel free to play around with it and see how the sample size, the computed average, and the null hypothesis values impact our confidence in the decision to reject H_0.

Determining the P-value

The p-value is a term that often comes up in articles, documentaries, and reports. However, it can be challenging to grasp what it means and why it is useful. Using the tools we have studied in this chapter, we should be able to make sense of it.

To start, we will revisit the alpha value, which helped us draw the line of how unlikely a value needs to be to reject the null hypothesis. In a right-tailed test, the alpha value defines the shaded area under the normal curve shown in Figure 5-6.

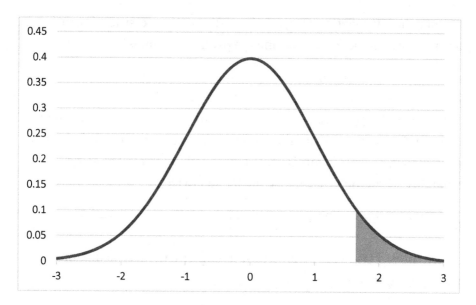

Figure 5-6. *In a right-tailed test, we need our test statistic to be sufficiently far from the mean (on the horizontal X axis) so that it enters the orange-shaded area. We define the size of that area with the alpha value*

Figure 5-6 makes it visually clear that the alpha value separates the "most extreme" values from the rest of the distribution. If this were a left-tailed test, the shaded area would instead be on the left-hand side of the distribution, while a two-tailed test would have shaded areas on both sides.

To reject the null hypothesis, we want our test statistic to fall within the shaded area. It needs to be extreme enough to reject the probability that this distribution produced it by random chance. The p-value is the probability of obtaining a value that is at least as extreme as our own. For the right-tailed test depicted in Figure 5-6, we would write

$$P-Value = P\left[X > \bar{x}\right] = 1 - P\left[X < \bar{x}\right] = 1 - CDF_{N(\mu,\sigma)}\left(\bar{x}\right)$$

Since the left-tailed test regards the left side of the distribution as extreme, the formula for computing the p-value becomes

$$P-Value = P\left[X < \overline{x}\right] = CDF_{N(\mu,\sigma)}\left(\overline{x}\right)$$

The formula for the two-tailed test is a little trickier since we need to take both sides of the distribution into account. However, the distribution we are working with is symmetric, and both tails will have the same probability. Therefore, we can use the left tail twice:

$$P-Value = 2 \cdot P\left[X < \mu - |\mu - \overline{x}|\right] = 2 \cdot CDF_{N(\mu,\sigma)}\left(\mu - |\mu - \overline{x}|\right)$$

The code in Listing 5-4 shows how to implement this calculation in an easy-to-use function.

Listing 5-4. Computing the p-value using Swift

```
enum TestTail {
  case left, right, both
}

func pValue(
  of x: Double,
  mu: Double,
  sigma: Double,
  tail: TestTail
) -> Double {

  let dist = NormalDistribution(
    mean: mu,
    standardDeviation: sigma
  )
```

```
  let leftProb = dist.cdf(x: mu - abs(mu - x))
  return tail == .both
    ? 2 * leftProb
    : leftProb
}

let sample = 105.0
let mu = 100.0
let sigma = 15 / sqrt(30)
let pValue = pValue(
  of: sample,
  mu: mu,
  sigma: sigma,
  tail: .right
)

print("P-Value for the dean's experiment: \(pValue)")

// Prints:
// P-Value for the dean's experiment:
// 0.033944520649489496
```

Standardization

One common way of dealing with hypothesis testing is to standardize the test statistic. That is, we transform it in such a way that we compare it to some standard distribution. Chapter 3 mentioned the standard normal distribution – a normal distribution with a mean of zero and a standard deviation of one. It would be fantastic if we could always use the same set of parameters to test our hypothesis. The main gain would be that an alpha value would draw the rejection line at the same X-axis value every time instead of depending on the exact shape of the distribution. Luckily for us, there exists such a standardization.

Computing a Standard Score

A standard score, also called a z-score, is a compact formula that transforms our observed value into a standardized number. It represents the number of standard deviations that the raw score differs from the mean. If we standardize a raw score from another normal distribution, it could also be considered as transforming the raw score and the original distribution to a standard normal distribution. Figure 5-7 shows a conceptual image of this line of thought.

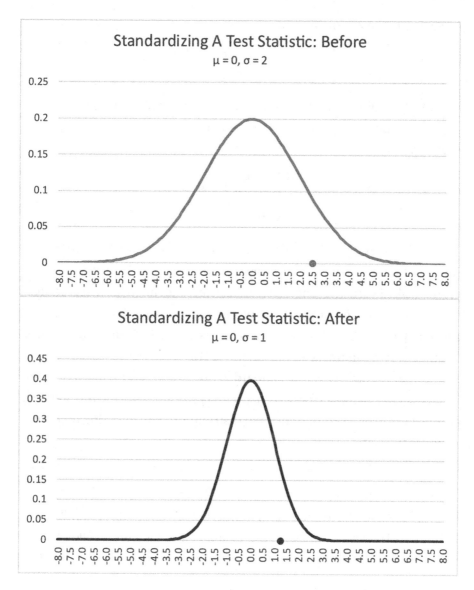

Figure 5-7. *The z-score conceptualized as transforming a raw score and its original normal distribution into a standard normal distribution*

We define the z-score as

$$z = \frac{x - \mu}{\sigma}$$

In this formula, μ and σ are the mean and standard deviation of the population. Computing the z-score for the intelligence tests from before, we end up with

$$\frac{105 - 100}{\frac{15}{\sqrt{30}}} \approx 1.826$$

This z-score tells us that the average result that the students produced is about 1.8 standard deviations away from the mean of the distribution. Now the task of verifying whether we can reject the null hypothesis comes down to comparing it to the z-score of some alpha value. For example, a right-tailed test alpha value of 0.05 has a z-score of 1.645. Since our statistic has a higher score in this test, we can reject H_0.

Now that we have covered standardization and z-scores, feel free to go back to the code samples for this chapter. Try normalizing the test statistic, running it through a standard normal distribution, and ensuring that the results are the same.

Note   The results may differ slightly when using the z-score. This difference comes from rounding errors related to the limited bitwidth of computers. However, the errors are so small that they are negligible.

Computing Confidence Intervals

Not only does the z-score provide a way to use the same measuring tape for our tests, regardless of from which distribution our data came. It also provides a way to learn precisely how confident we are in our results.

Revisiting the students at the university, we want to know how far off our estimate of their mean intelligence score might be. That is, we want to know the range of μ that solves the following probability:

$$P\left[-z < \frac{x-\mu}{\sigma} < z\right] = c = 1-\alpha$$

By doing some algebraic manipulations of this expression, we can rewrite it to become

$$P[\mu - z\sigma < x < \mu + z\sigma] = c = 1-\alpha$$

Since we can easily find out which z values correspond to different confidence levels or alpha values and are only interested in the limiting values of μ this expression, we can further rewrite this equation to

$$\mu_{1,2} = x \pm z\sigma$$

This expression looks tiny, but it is all we need to compute a confidence interval for our result. Since our sample mean and the population's standard deviation are constants, the only knob we need to turn is the one for z. Let us say that we want to know the range in which our sample mean falls with 95% certainty. Because this is a two-tailed calculation, we need to take equally much of the uncertainty into account on each side, which means that we need to divide the alpha value by two. The z-score that corresponds to an alpha value of 0.025 is 1.96. Therefore, we get the following:

$$\mu_{1,2} = 105 \pm 1.96 \cdot \frac{15}{\sqrt{30}} \approx 105 \pm 5.37$$

This result yields a range from 99.63 to 110.37, and we can therefore be 95% sure that our students' true mean intelligence score is somewhere between those numbers. This technique is powerful since it gives us a tool to determine where the sample mean might end up if we were to perform this test from the start.

A Word on Chi-Squared Tests

Chi-squared tests are another helpful category of hypothesis tests that can help us determine, for example, how well some measured data fits a model. We perform these tests with methodologies that are very similar to the ones we have talked about in this chapter – we set up null and alternative hypotheses, decide on an alpha value, and perform the test. However, to fully understand how and why these tests are useful, we need to understand how the chi-squared distribution works, which could probably fill another chapter on its own. Nevertheless, feel free to take a closer look at these topics as a part of further studies.

Chapter Summary

This chapter was quite heavy on the theory side. We learned what a hypothesis is and how to formulate both null and alternative hypotheses for our tests. We learned about the distribution of sample means and got introduced to one of the most important theorems in statistics – the Central Limit Theorem. We learned how to define confidence levels, alpha values, and compute p-values, and we also had a look at how to standardize a test statistic and compute confidence intervals for it.

The next chapter will make a complete U-turn. The theoretical concepts will be lighter and intuitive to grasp, and we will focus more on the code part of things. It has come time to learn how to shrink information with statistics.

CHAPTER 6

Statistical Methods for Data Compression

Statistical methods are not only applicable in hardcore data science topics. They also have applications in what could be considered more traditional computer science, such as compression algorithms. While there is active research conducted in compression via machine learning, we will explore, derive, and implement a much more medieval, rule-based algorithm.

An Introduction to Compression

The concept of compression is straightforward when looking at it from a high-level perspective. We want to transform some arbitrary piece of data so that it takes up less space. The less space this data occupies, the more space we will have for other data later. We call this transformation for *compression*.

Not only do we want some algorithm that makes our data smaller in size. We also want this process to be reversible in some sense. Once we have found a representation that takes up less space, we want to have the option to get back the original data. This reversion of the compression stage is called *decompression*.

As an example, let us analyze a simple compression algorithm. Whenever someone hands us a block of data, we always return a single byte with the value 0xFF. When we look at the compression stage, this algorithm is doing amazing things. We could hand it Netflix's entire

© Jimmy Andersson 2022
J. Andersson, *Statistical Analysis with Swift*, https://doi.org/10.1007/978-1-4842-7765-2_6

video library, and it would be able to compress it to a single byte. That is impressive! However, things look pretty bleak when we move to the decompression stage. The algorithm always returns the same compressed representation, no matter the input. If someone handed us that byte and told us to decompress it, we would not know whether to turn it into an animated movie, a digital restaurant menu, or the Bill of Rights. That is a horrible property! To get this right, we need to discuss a few mathematical properties related to functions.

Function Behaviors

As many of us are probably already aware, a mathematical function is a way of mapping the members of an input set called the *domain* to the members of an output set called the *range*. Every element in the domain needs to map to a single element in the range. If a domain member has multiple mappings or no mapping, it is not a function in the mathematical sense. Figure 6-1 shows an example of a mapping that does not qualify as a function.

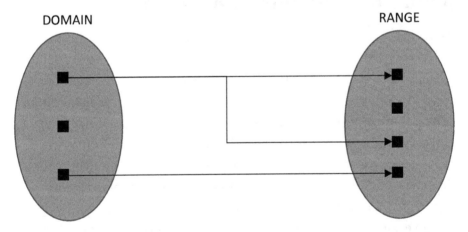

Figure 6-1. *This mapping does not qualify as a function. Not all domain members have a mapping to a range element, while others have multiple mappings*

Now that we know how mathematicians define a function, we can discuss some different properties of these mappings. Given that we have a function $f(x)$ that maps the elements of a domain X to some range Y, we say that

- The function $f(x)$ is **surjective** if all elements in Y are mapped by some element in X. The nice thing with this type of function is that all elements of the set Y are reached by some element in X. However, surjective functions allow that multiple domain members map to the same range member, so different inputs might yield the same output.

- The function $f(x)$ is **injective** if a member of the range Y can only be mapped by a single element in X. A function with this property never maps two different inputs to the same output. However, there may be elements in the range that are not mapped at all, so we may not be able to backtrack and find the input element if someone gave us an output element.

- A function $f(x)$ that is both surjective and injective is called **bijective**. A bijective function maps all elements in the domain to a different element in the range, so there is a perfect one-to-one mapping. A handy property of bijective functions is that there exists an inverse function $f-1(x)$ that maps the elements in Y back to their corresponding elements in X.

Let us look at an example to get an intuition of what this means. We define the function:

$$f(x) = x^2, \quad x \in \mathbb{R}$$

The function $f(x)$ has a domain that spans the entire real number line. Given that it can only ever yield nonnegative numbers, its range consists of the nonnegative real numbers. This function is surjective since $f(x)$ can produce any nonnegative real value from all the possible inputs. However, the function is not injective. That is, the function does not produce unique results for all the elements of the domain. One example is that -1 and 1 produce the same result. Thanks to this, the function is not bijective either. We can map all possible inputs to the output space in a well-defined way, but we do not have an inverse function that takes us back to the original input with certainty.

Now, take the following function instead:

$$f(x) = x + 2, \quad x \in \mathbb{R}$$

The real numbers constitute both the domain and the range of this function. We can see that it is surjective since it maps all members of the range. It is also an injective function since all domain elements produce unique results. Since $f(x)$ is both injective and surjective, it is also bijective, and we can find an inverse function $f^{-1}(x)$ by doing some algebraic manipulations.

$$f(x) = y$$
$$f^{-1}(y) = x$$

$$f(x) = x + 2$$
$$y = x + 2$$
$$x = y - 2$$
$$f^{-1}(y) = y - 2$$

Given this theory, bijection is a desirable property for a compression algorithm. When we change the representation of some data, often into a format that is not particularly human readable, we want to be able to invert that compression and get back the original information. However, there are times when we are okay with the function only being "approximately bijective," which is a fascinating subject that we will discuss next.

Lossless vs. Lossy Compression

One crucial aspect of any compression algorithm is whether it is lossy or lossless. That is, do we get the same data back when we decompress it, or does it differ? Let us look at Figure 6-2 to see a visualization of a truly bijective compression algorithm.

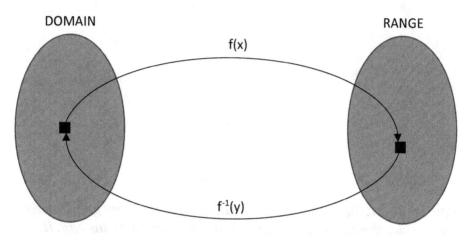

Figure 6-2. *The function used to compress a data point in the domain has an inverse that allows us to get back the exact same information when decompressing*

The compression function visualized in Figure 6-2 is bijective, which means that the decompression function will give us back the exact same data we compressed. Algorithms that display this behavior are commonly called lossless. Some examples of formats that use lossless compression are

- bzip2 (general purpose)
- FLAC (audio)
- WMA Lossless (audio)
- PNG (graphics)

On the opposite side, we have compression functions that are only "approximately bijective." Although this is not a commonly accepted term, it quite accurately describes the behavior we are after. Figure 6-3 shows the idea behind such a function.

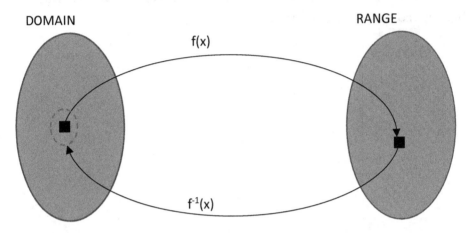

Figure 6-3. *An "approximately bijective" function is not guaranteed to reproduce the exact same data when decompressing. Instead, it will produce an approximation of that data point – one close to the original by some distance measure of our choice*

We commonly refer to this type of function as lossy compression. Suppose we can live with the fact that we probably will not be able to reproduce the original data again. In that case, a lossy compression algorithm can often come up with a data representation that takes less space than a lossless algorithm could. Some popular file formats that use lossy compression algorithms include

- MP3 (audio)

- WMA (audio)

- JPEG (graphics)

- H.261 (graphics)

Now that we know more about some of the important compression characteristics, we will dive deeper by implementing a lossless algorithm based on Huffman Coding.

Huffman Coding

David A. Huffman is the father of the Huffman algorithm. The general idea of this algorithm is to generate a sequence of zeros and ones to represent some element in a distribution. The sequences fulfill a few requirements:

1. The sequence must be unique for each unique element in the distribution.

2. The more common an element is, the shorter the sequence should be that represents it.

3. The sequences we decide on should minimize the expected sequence length over the distribution of elements. That is, we want to minimize the total length of all sequences needed to represent the complete data set.

Let us look at producing Huffman codes for each letter in the word "Hello" to gain some intuition. Table 6-1 shows the frequencies of each letter.

Table 6-1. *The letter frequencies of the word "Hello"*

Letter	Frequency
H	1
E	1
L	2
O	1

Table 6-1 shows that the letter l is the most common, while the others are equally frequent. Therefore, it is more important that a shorter sequence represents l than any other letter. The Huffman algorithm generates these sequences by building a binary tree from the following steps:

1. View each element and its associated count as leaf nodes in a tree.

2. Find the two nodes that are the least frequent. If there are several with the same frequency, pick one at random.

3. Group the two nodes as children of a new tree node. The frequency of the new node is the sum of the frequency of its children.

4. Put the new node back into the collection.

5. If there is still more than one node left in the collection, go back to step 2. If only a single node is left, it represents our Huffman tree, and we can stop.

Following this algorithm, the word "Hello" produces a tree similar to Figure 6-4.

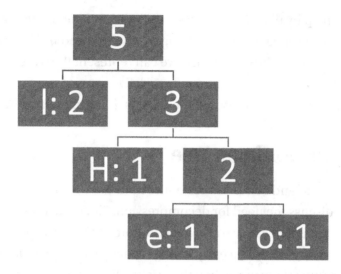

Figure 6-4. *An example of a Huffman tree for the word "Hello." Leaf nodes show both the represented letter and frequency count, while branch nodes show the total frequency inherited from their children*

Now that we have built our Huffman tree, we can produce codes for each leaf node. Let us decide that moving down a left branch appends a 0 to our code sequence while taking the right branch appends a 1. Since we only need to move down a single left branch to get to the letter "l", it can be represented by the code "0". However, the letter "e" is located further down the tree and therefore needs the longer sequence "110". We list all the Huffman codes generated by this tree in Table 6-2.

Table 6-2. *All Huffman codes generated by the tree shown in Figure 6-4*

Letter	Huffman Code
H	10
E	110
L	0
O	111

We finish up by placing the codes to follow the same sequential ordering as the original letters. By doing so, "Hello" becomes "10 110 0 0 111". Thanks to the Huffman codes, we can represent the word "Hello" using only ten bits. A word that initially took five bytes of storage only takes two bytes with the new representation. That is quite an improvement!

Storing the Huffman Tree

Before we run off and compress our entire hard drive into Huffman codes, we need to discuss the need for decompression. Since we want to recreate the original data perfectly, we also need to store the tree used to compress it. However, doing so also takes up storage space. In our example, we will probably end up taking more than the original five bytes once we save the tree. If that is the case, then what is the point of doing all of this?

Because of the learning nature of the example, we wanted the data to be small. Real-life use cases hardly ever include compressing a text file containing a single word. Instead, we may want to compress large video files or log files with millions of lines. The space used to store the Huffman tree becomes negligible as the size of the data set grows. For example, if we save a couple of hundred megabytes compressing a massive file, there is no harm in using a couple of extra kilobytes for the tree.

Note   The Huffman tree we computed in the previous example is not a unique optimal solution. Depending on the method we use to break ties, we may also end up with a tree that produces four codes of length 2. They both minimize the expected number of bits used to represent our word, but it is good to keep in mind that some inputs may have multiple optimal Huffman code sets.

Implementing a Compression Algorithm

Now that we have covered the concepts of Huffman codes, we will spend the remainder of the chapter implementing a compression algorithm that builds on these ideas. The implementation will cover all the steps needed to produce a Huffman tree, compress a string of Lorem Ipsum text, and put it in a binary object together with the tree. It will also cover the reverse, in which we parse a Huffman tree and some compressed text from a binary representation. While the compressed text is encoded to be as space efficient as possible, we will not make the same effort to minimize the tree's memory footprint. However, using the same techniques that we use to encode the Huffman codes, we could certainly reduce the tree's space requirements, too!

The Compression Stage

Let us start by looking at the main program used to compress some text, shown in Listing 6-1.

Listing 6-1. The main program used to compress some example text

```
let text = DataLoader.loadText(from: .huffman)
let coder = HuffmanTextCoder()
let compressed = try coder.encode(text)
```

This program is relatively small since all the complexity is tucked away inside the HuffmanTextCoder instance. We use an alternative load function from the DataLoader to read a text file located in the shared resources of the code project. We then pass the loaded text into the encode(_:) function, which returns a compressed binary representation in the form of a Data object.

To encode a text string, we first need to decide on how to subdivide our data points. There are many ways in which we could split the text. Should we split it into sentences, words, or perhaps letters? For this implementation, we choose to go with bytes. Therefore, the Huffman tree will construct codes for all the eight-bit patterns used to construct the UTF-8 coded string, and the steps needed to encode the compressed data can be summarized as follows:

1. Count the frequency of each byte in the text to find the distribution.

2. Construct a Huffman tree from the counts extracted in step 1.

3. Create a binary representation of the tree to store with the compressed text.

4. Create a Huffman code representation of the text with the tree created in step 2.

5. Concatenate the binary version of the Huffman tree and the compressed text into a single binary object.

Listing 6-2 shows the encode(_:) function, which delegates each step above to separate, specialized methods. Listing 6-3 displays an enumeration we use in the case of encoding or decoding failures. While we do not use the enum explicitly inside this method, it is good to know the different types of errors the subroutines can throw from the call marked with the try keyword.

Listing 6-2. Our implementation of HuffmanTextCoder.encode(_:)

```
func encode(_ text: String) throws -> Data {
  let byteFrequencies = countBytes(in: text)

  let root = try createHuffmanTree(
```

```
    from: byteFrequencies
  )

  let treeData = createTreeData(from: root)

  var (encodedText, encodingSize) = try encodeText(
    text,
    with: root,
    frequencies: byteFrequencies
  )

  let encodingSizeData = Data(
    bytes: &encodingSize,
    count: MemoryLayout<Int>.size
  )

  return encodingSizeData + treeData + encodedText
}
```

Listing 6-3. An enumeration used to represent errors that may be thrown during compression or decompression

```
enum HuffmanError: Error {
  case emptyInputData
  case treeBuilderFailure
  case textEncodingFailure
  case textDecodingFailure
}
```

As Listing 6-2 shows, we walk through each step that we lined out earlier. However, there is one variable in the code that we did not yet discuss, namely, encodingSize. It is generated by the method that encodes the text into Huffman coded binary data, and its purpose is to let us know how many bits we used to encode the entire message.

Since the smallest addressable building block in a general-purpose computer is a byte, that limits us to working with multiples of eight bits. However, it is much more likely that we will need some off-sized number of bits. For example, we needed ten bits to encode the word "Hello," which requires us to allocate two bytes. Those two bytes contain 16 bits, which means that we will end up with six unused bits in the encoded data. Now imagine decoding those two bytes of data and not knowing how many bits contain useful information. We would decide the first ten bits correctly. However, we would also decode the last six bits, ultimately ending up with the word "Hellollllll". Since that is not what we want, we need to hint at when to stop the decoding process. Instead of inventing a stop sequence, we simply prepend the number of bits to the beginning of the encoded data.

Now that we know what the final binary object will look like, let us dig deeper into the different subroutines that will make this happen. Listing 6-4 shows the method countBytes(in:), which is in charge of computing the distribution of bytes in the text.

Listing 6-4. The implementation of countBytes(in:), which returns the distribution of bytes inside a text string

```swift
func countBytes(in text: String) -> [UInt8: Int] {
  var text = text

  return text.withUTF8 { pointer in
    pointer
      .reduce(into: [UInt8: Int]()) { dict, byte in
        dict[byte, default: 0] += 1
      }
  }
}
```

The first thing that happens in the preceding method is that we make the text parameter mutable. Since we do not plan on mutating the string, this is not a hard requirement from the algorithms side. Instead, it is a requirement imposed by the String type itself. Since a pointer to the contents of a string will allow us to mutate whatever is in there, we cannot use it on an immutable object.

Next, we request a pointer to a contiguous block of memory holding the byte contents of the text. Once that is given to us, we can count each byte by using a higher-order function. The method reduce(into:_:) will take each byte in the storage and use it to increment a counter. When the iteration finishes, we return a Dictionary containing the bytes and their respective counter variables. We represent bytes using the type UInt8, so if we feed the word "Hello" into countBytes(in:), it will yield something similar to[111: 1, 108: 2, 101: 1, 72: 1]. In this particular case, the bytes correspond perfectly to the ASCII code representations of the individual letters. However, that might not always be the case since we are working with UTF-8 encoded strings.

Next, we move on to look at createHuffmanTree(from:), which builds a Huffman tree from the distribution we just computed. Listing 6-5 shows the enum we use to represent a node in the tree, while Listing 6-6 shows the method implementation.

Listing 6-5. The HuffmanNode enumeration we use to represent a tree node

```
indirect enum HuffmanNode<Value>
where Value: Hashable & Comparable {
  case node(left: HuffmanNode, right: HuffmanNode)
  case leaf(value: Value, count: Int)
}
```

Listing 6-6. Our implementation of createHuffmanTree(from:)

```
func createHuffmanTree(from freqs: [UInt8: Int])
throws -> HuffmanNode<UInt8> {
  var nodes = freqs
    .map { key, value -> HuffmanNode in
      .leaf(value: key, count: value)
    }
    .sorted(by: >)

  guard !nodes.isEmpty else {
    throw HuffmanError.emptyInputData
  }

  while
    nodes.count > 1,
    let rhs = nodes.popLast(),
    let lhs = nodes.popLast()
  {
    nodes.append(.node(left: lhs, right: rhs))
    nodes.sort(by: >)
  }

  if let root = nodes.first {
    return root
  } else {
    throw HuffmanError.treeBuilderFailure
  }
}
```

A few interesting things are happening in these snippets. First off, the HuffmanNode enum is a generic type that allows us to create a tree over any other type, so long as it conforms to the Hashable protocol and the Comparable protocol.

Secondly, we have marked the HuffmanNode with the indirect keyword. This keyword is a construct that is not very common to see out in the wild at the time of writing. However, it allows an enumeration to reference itself recursively. Before indirect came about, developers were not allowed to use value types to create graph-like structures. This limitation stemmed from the compiler and how it computed the memory footprint of different types. If a value type referenced itself, the compiler would think it needed infinite memory to store an instance. Thanks to the indirect keyword, we are now allowed to use enums like this. However, structs still throw a compilation error.

The algorithm that creates the tree starts by mapping the bytes and their respective counts to one leaf node each. It then builds a full tree by grouping the two smallest nodes into a new branch node until only a single node remains in the collection – the root node.

One important thing to note is that we need the HuffmanNode instances to conform to the Comparable protocol if we want to sort them. We want to order the nodes according to their frequency count. If their counts are equal, we instead order them according to the byte value. This fallback behavior is not strictly necessary but will break ties in a predictive way, making sure that a text generates the same Huffman tree every time we run the algorithm. Listing 6-7 and the HuffmanNode+Comparable.swift file in the code project show the implementations needed to conform to the Comparable protocol.

Listing 6-7. Conforming our HuffmanNodes to the Comparable protocol

```
extension HuffmanNode: Comparable {
  static func < (
    lhs: HuffmanNode<Value>,
    rhs: HuffmanNode<Value>
  ) -> Bool {
```

```
    switch (lhs, rhs) {
      case (.leaf(let lhsValue, let lhsCount),
            .leaf(let rhsValue, let rhsCount)):
        return lhsCount == rhsCount
          ? lhsValue < rhsValue
          : lhsCount < rhsCount
      default:
        return lhs.count < rhs.count
    }
  }

  static func == (
    lhs: HuffmanNode<Value>,
    rhs: HuffmanNode<Value>
  ) -> Bool {
    switch (lhs, rhs) {
      case (.node(let lhsleft, let lhsright),
            .node(let rhsleft, let rhsright)):
        return
          lhsleft == rhsleft &&
          lhsright == rhsright

      case (.leaf(let lhsValue, let lhsCount),
            .leaf(let rhsValue, let rhsCount)):
        return
          lhsValue == rhsValue &&
          lhsCount == rhsCount
      default:
        return false
    }
  }
}
```

Now that we have a Huffman tree, it has come time to encode both it and the text into binary representations. We start by encoding the tree, using the method createTreeData(from:) shown in Listing 6-8.

Listing 6-8. Encoding our Huffman tree into a binary representation that can be stored with the compressed text

```
func createTreeData(
  from node: HuffmanNode<UInt8>
) -> Data {
  switch node {
    case .node(let lhs, let rhs):
      let left = createTreeData(from: lhs)
      let right = createTreeData(from: rhs)
      let branchMarker = Data(repeating: 0, count: 1)
      return branchMarker + left + right

    case .leaf(var value, var count):
      let valueData = Data(
        bytes: &value,
        count: MemoryLayout<UInt8>.size
      )
      let countData = Data(
        bytes: &count,
        count: MemoryLayout<Int>.size
      )
      let leafMarker = Data(repeating: 1, count: 1)
      return leafMarker + countData + valueData
  }
}
```

The recursive nature of `createTreeData(from:)` makes it a pretty compact method. The general idea comes down to the following:

- If a leaf node is sent into the function, we simply return a binary package consisting of a leaf node marker, the frequency count, and the byte associated with the node.

- If a branch node is passed into the function, we know that we have access to two child nodes. We encode them by passing them into a recursive method call, and then we return a branch node marker, followed by the data returned by the left node and the right node, respectively. Since all paths down the tree are guaranteed to hit a leaf node, we can be sure that the recursion terminates at some finite point in time.

As we mentioned earlier, this part of the implementation has room for improvement if one wants to save even more space. Each marker adds an entire byte to the data object, even though we could technically represent it using a single bit. With a little bit of work and creative thinking, one could re-implement `createTreeData(from:)` using the same ideas we will see in the following method. Listing 6-9 shows the implementation of en codeText(_:with:frequencies:), which creates a compressed binary representation of our text.

Listing 6-9. Encoding a text string using the computed Huffman tree

```
func encodeText(
    _ text: String,
    with root: HuffmanNode<UInt8>,
    frequencies: [UInt8: Int]
) throws -> (data: Data, numberOfBits: Int) {
```

```
let codes = root.codeMap()
let numberOfBits = frequencies
  .reduce(into: 0) { result, args in
    let (byte, count) = args
    let mapping = codes[byte, default: (Data(), 0)]
    result += mapping.bitLength * count
  }
let numberOfBytes = 1 + (numberOfBits - 1) / 8
var encoding = Data(
  repeating: 0,
  count: numberOfBytes
)

var textVar = text
var index = 0
try textVar.withUTF8 { pointer in
  try pointer.forEach { byte in
    guard let (bits, bitCount) = codes[byte]
    else { throw HuffmanError.textEncodingFailure }
    for offset in 0 ..< bitCount {
      let mask: UInt8 = 0x80 >> (offset % 8)
      let masked = bits[offset / 8] & mask
      if masked > 0 {
        encoding[index / 8] |= 0x80 >> (index % 8)
      }
      index += 1
    }
  }
}
return (encoding, numberOfBits)
}
```

This function utilizes lower-level programming concepts such as bitwise operations, and there is an endless sea of details that we could spend another book discussing. However, to get the general ideas across, we will keep the discussion on a higher level. Feel free to experiment with the implementation in the code project since that will give a deeper understanding of the small details.

First, encodeText(_:with:frequencies:) asks the Huffman tree we computed to create a map of all the codes. We will not go through the codeMap() method in detail since it merely reduces the Huffman codes into a Dictionary format. The type annotation of the code map is [UInt8: (Data, Int)] and maps each byte to its respective Huffman code and the length of the code.

In the next step, we compute the total number of bits needed to encode the text. We also translate the number of bits into the corresponding number of bytes and allocate as much memory as we need to represent the encoded text.

Like before, we will need a pointer to the original text and need to create a mutable version of it. We take care of that by storing it in a new textVar variable. We also create a counter variable, index, to track which bit we are currently encoding. Now, the idea is to iterate over the bytes in the text, retrieve the Huffman code for it, and write each one or zero into the new storage. The for loops are pretty straightforward, but let us take a closer look at the bitwise operations.

The mask variable creates a bitmask that targets a single bit in the Huffman code. We then use the mask to compute the masked variable, which is zero if the targeted Huffman code bit is zero and nonzero if the code bit is one. Since we initialized the encoding storage to all zeros, we only need to write a bit if the masked variable is greater than zero. At the end of the iteration, we increment the index variable to indicate that we are ready to move on to the next bit.

The function later returns the encoding object and the number of bits we used to encode the text, just like we discussed before. All we have to do at this point is to concatenate our computations in the correct order and return it to the call site. Inside the main script, we can print the size of the original text and the size of the compressed data to see the difference, like shown in Listing 6-10.

Listing 6-10. Comparing the size of the original text and the representation produced by our algorithm

```
print(
    """
    Text size: \(text.utf8.count) bytes
    Data size: \(compressed.count) bytes
    """
)

// Prints:
// Text size: 12806 bytes
// Data size: 7331 bytes
```

The compressed data takes less than 60% of the original storage. That is impressive, especially since we have already concluded that this representation encodes the Huffman tree in a nonoptimal way.

Now that we can compress an arbitrary text string, we need to devise an algorithm that reverses the process. The following section will discuss and create an algorithm to decompress the bits and turn them into UTF-8 bytes.

The Decompression Stage

Before we dive into implementing a decompression algorithm, let us take a step back and analyze the structure of the data object we have encoded.

- Four or eight bytes specify the number of bits used to encode the text. The exact number of bytes is dependent on our platform. On 32-bit platforms, Int takes 4 bytes, while it takes 8 bytes on 64-bit platforms.

- Some arbitrary number of bytes define the Huffman tree we used to encode the original text. While we may not know precisely how many bytes it consists of, we know that it starts right after the bytes that specify bitlength, and we know that it is structured in a fashion that allows recursive unpacking.

- Another arbitrary number of bytes contains the encoded message. We can compute its start location in memory by calculating the size of the two previous data sections and can extract all the remaining data from there.

By splitting the workload into methods that deal with the different data sections we specified earlier, we can define a decode(_:) method that assembles the original text from a Data object. Listing 6-11 shows an implementation of this.

Listing 6-11. Our implementation of HuffmanTextCoder.decode(_:)

```
func decode(_ data: Data) throws -> String {
  let encodingSize = parseEncodingBitSize(data)

  var huffmanData = data[MemoryLayout<Int>.size...]
  let tree = parseTree(&huffmanData)
```

```
let text = try parseText(
  from: huffmanData,
  using: tree,
  bitLength: encodingSize
)

return text
}
```

The code shown in Listing 6-11 perfectly reflects the parsing of different sections of data listed on the previous page. The abstractions make it easier to get an overview of the steps and allow us to focus on a single task at a time. However, it does not provide any more profound understanding of what is going on in the background, so we have to dive deeper. Listing 6-12 shows parseEncodingBitSize(_:), which reads the length of the encoded text.

Listing 6-12. Our implementation of parseEncodingBitSize(_:)

```
func parseEncodingBitSize(_ data: Data) -> Int {
  data.withUnsafeBytes { pointer in
    pointer.load(as: Int.self)
  }
}
```

To parse the number of bits used to encode the original text, we want to read the first four or eight bytes from the compressed data. Asking a data object for a pointer is relatively straightforward. Because we are only interested in reading the contents without mutating them, we use the withUnsafeBytes(_:) method, which provides access to a read-only buffer pointer. If we wanted a mutating pointer, we would create a mutable variable and use withUnsafeMutableBytes(_:).

The pointer we get back is an `UnsafeRawBufferPointer`, which has two important properties. First, it does not carry any type information. That is the nature of a raw pointer; it has no idea of what kind of content it holds. Second, it conforms to the `Collection` protocol, which gives us access to many valuable operations such as subscripts, element counts, and indices.

To parse the bit count, we use the function `load(fromByteOffset:as:)`, which parses the number of bytes that make up an `Int` starting at the offset we provide. In our case, we use the default value of 0 for `fromByteOffset`, and we can therefore leave out that parameter.

Now that we have decoded the first piece of data, it is time to decode the Huffman tree. We create a mutable variable called `huffmanData`, which contains all but the bytes that we just parsed. We pass the new data object into the `parseTree(_:)` function, for which we show the implementation in Listing 6-13.

Listing 6-13. The implementation of parseTree(_:)

```
func parseTree(
    _ data: inout Data
) -> HuffmanNode<UInt8> {

  let marker = data.first
  data = Data(data.dropFirst())

  switch marker {
    case 0:
      let left = parseTree(&data)
      let right = parseTree(&data)
      return .node(left: left, right: right)

    default:
      let (count, value) = data
        .withUnsafeBytes { pointer -> (Int, UInt8) in
```

```
    let count = pointer.load(as: Int.self)
    let value = pointer.load(
      fromByteOffset: MemoryLayout<Int>.size,
      as: UInt8.self
    )
    return (count, value)
  }

  let intSize = MemoryLayout<Int>.size
  let byteSize = MemoryLayout<UInt8>.size
  data = Data(data.dropFirst(intSize + byteSize))

  return .leaf(value: value, count: count)
}
}
```

This method starts by fetching the first byte from the data object, which contains a marker telling us whether we are parsing a branch node or a leaf node. It then creates a new Data object by dropping the marker byte. Creating many new objects like this is generally frowned upon since it can impose a significant performance hit. The question is, why do we do it then?

The fact that we need to create a new Data object is a side effect of how we packed our tree. On the one hand, we stored the markers, byte values, and counts in a compact way. It was not as compact as possible, but there were no gaps between the different pieces of information. On the other hand, this way of packing different types violates some alignment conventions. For example, the UInt8 type has an alignment of 1. If we store a UInt8 value at offset 0, then the next legal offset to store another UInt8 value is 0 + 1 = 1. For Int64, the corresponding alignment is 8. Such a value is only legal if we store it at an offset which is a multiple of 8, such as 0, 8, or 16. Herein lies a problem with our compact representation. We store a

UInt8-sized marker at offset 0 and an Int-sized count variable at offset 1. To solve this misalignment problem, we create a new Data object, which effectively resets the offset and puts the first element at index 0.

Note   As previously mentioned, it is entirely possible to store the tree differently. One could throw away the count variable as a simple fix since it is not pertinent to the decoding process. That would eradicate the alignment issue since the rest of the encoded data is of type UInt8. Feel free to play around with the code project and see which other solutions are possible.

Now that we know about potential issues when encoding binary data like this, let us look at the rest of parseTree(_:). We switch on the marker to determine if the current node is a branch or a leaf. If the node is a branch, we recursively call parseTree(_:) to decode the left and right branches and return them grouped under a new .node instance. If, on the other hand, we are parsing a leaf node, we read out the count and byte value from the pointer. We then resolve any future alignment issues by creating a new Data object, thereby resetting the indices after the node we just parsed. Finally, we return the leaf.

Last but not least, we look at the function that parses the encoded text message. Listing 6-14 shows the implementation.

Listing 6-14. Implementation of parseText(from:using:bitLength:)

```
func parseText(
  from data: Data,
  using tree: HuffmanNode<UInt8>,
  bitLength: Int
) throws -> String {
  var textData = Data()
```

```swift
  if case .leaf(let value, _) = tree {
    textData.append(
      contentsOf: [UInt8](
        repeating: value,
        count: bitLength
      )
    )
  } else {
    var index = 0
    var currentNode = tree
    while index <= bitLength {
      switch currentNode {
        case .leaf(let value, _):
          textData.append(value)
          currentNode = tree

        case .node(let lhs, let rhs):
          let mask = UInt8(0x80) >> (index % 8)
          let step = data[index / 8] & mask
          currentNode = step > 0 ? rhs : lhs
          index += 1
      }
    }
  }
  guard let text = String(
      data: textData,
      encoding: .utf8
    )
  else { throw HuffmanError.textDecodingFailure }
  return text
}
```

The first part of `parseText(from:using:bitLength:)` checks for a somewhat unusual but still important edge case. If the original text only consisted of one single byte value, for example, if it were just a file full of Ts, the tree would be a single leaf node. If that is the case, we should produce a `Data` object that repeats a single byte `bitLength` times. However, if the root is a branch node, we need to compute the correct byte orders by parsing individual bits.

We initialize an index variable that tracks which bit we are currently parsing. We also initialize a variable that allows us to traverse the tree according to the value of each bit. If we hit a leaf node, we append the byte value to a byte buffer named `textData`. However, if we hit a branch node, we create a mask that targets the current bit and check whether it is a zero or a one. According to the rules we defined in the compression stage, we move along the left branch if the bit value is zero and to the right otherwise. At this point, we increment the `index` counter and move on to look at the next bit.

After parsing all bits, we have a `textData` buffer that includes the original text byte values in the correct order. From here, we can use the dedicated `String` type initializer, `init(data:encoding:)`, to turn the decompressed data into an actual text string and return it.

To ensure that the decompression stage produces the proper output, we can compare the original text with the one that has gone through our compression pipeline. Listing 6-15 shows the final part of the main script.

Listing 6-15. Comparing the decompressed output to the original text

```
let decompressed = try coder.decode(compressed)

print(
    """

  Decompressed text matches original:
  \(text == decompressed ? "YES" : "NO")
    """
)
```

```
// Prints:
// Decompressed text matches original:
// YES
```

Even though this is by no means a complete example of how much storage we can save, it still highlights that these techniques can produce some awe-inspiring results. If a simple implementation with the problems and caveats discussed here can produce a 40% reduction in size, one can imagine what a more optimized version could do.

Chapter Summary

This chapter put much focus on the implementation side. We learned about functions and some of their properties, such as surjection, injection, and bijection. We also introduced the technically incorrect notion of "approximate bijection," which can be used as a tool when exact inversion is not required.

We studied Huffman codes and how to produce them by using binary trees. There was also some discussion around the uniqueness of such codes, as multiple trees may minimize the number of bits needed to encode some data. Finally, we implemented a text compression tool that allowed us to compress and decompress a text file. In this process, we also covered some low-level computer science knowledge about memory layout and the implications of such layout rules.

In the following chapter, we will combine many of the concepts learned throughout this book to implement a movie recommender system.

CHAPTER 7

Statistical Methods in Recommender Systems

When we log on to a website or open an app, there is a good chance that statistical methods are working behind the scenes. They may be serving content that we are likely to engage with or showing products we may want to purchase. The common denominator for all of these algorithms is that they use past behaviors and known preferences to make statistical predictions of things that we would like. In this chapter, we will build a recommender system to suggest movies we might like.

Recommender Systems

A recommender system is, at its heart, a system that tries to predict a preference. These systems are prevalent in different kinds of webshops, social media platforms, and streaming services. Some examples of recommender systems in action follow:

- The Netflix main page suggests a batch of movies that we might enjoy.

- YouTube shows a list of video clips that might pique our interest.

© Jimmy Andersson 2022
J. Andersson, *Statistical Analysis with Swift*, https://doi.org/10.1007/978-1-4842-7765-2_7

- LinkedIn and Facebook show us suggestions of people we may want to connect with or befriend.

- Twitter shows posts from people we are not familiar with, but that tweet about things we might like.

- Amazon suggests additional products that we might be interested in buying.

The preceding examples are just a few of the most prominent examples, but the point is clear – recommender systems are everywhere, and they impact how we spend our time, money, and attention.

The Functions of Recommender Systems

There are many reasons why we developed recommender systems, and some of them are more obvious than others. Let us take a look at the *why* so that we can better reason about the *how* later.

First of all, good recommendations increase the likelihood of upsales. An online store that makes good suggestions about additional products is more likely to sell additional goods. For example, imagine that we place a TV in our shopping cart at an online electronics store. The store could make a little bit more money by suggesting a pack of batteries for the remote, some screen cleaner wipes, or a wall mount. Those all seem like good things to present to someone on their way to buy a television. However, they may not be so lucky if they show a computer or a coffee maker. Of course, the customer could also be looking for precisely those things, but that seems like an unsafe bet.

Secondly, good recommendations make the customer feel at home. We have all experienced the feeling when a website suggests that we purchase completely lunatic products. That feeling can even cause potential customers to leave the site and never return. A service that makes appropriate suggestions makes the user feel seen and understood, which makes the experience of using it that much better. By this logic, a sound recommender system serves both the company that sells products and the customers that use it. For example, Netflix would not have the same base of engaged viewers if their applications had just suggested random movies from any genre.

Approaching the Problem

Making suggestions like this is by no means an easy topic, and there is plenty of ongoing research in this area. This chapter will take a similar route as we did when deriving the formulas for linear regression. We will start with a simple but somewhat naive rule for making movie suggestions, discuss its implications, and improve it. In the end, we will land on a method called *collaborative filtering*, which we will implement to suggest movies for a user.

First Approach

Our first rule for suggesting movies is to pick some movies at random, regardless of their genre or rating. This rule is straightforward to reason about and implement, so it is attractive from a complexity viewpoint. However, there are some inherent problems with such an approach.

- We are equally likely to pick a movie with a bad rating as with a good rating. Thanks to this, we are likely to suggest a mix of movies that vary significantly in quality. Another issue comes around as we make more and more suggestions. Over time, the distribution of good and bad movies we suggest will tend toward the ratings of all available movies. This property means that if we have a greater number of bad movies available, we will suggest more bad movies than good ones. That is a real problem!

- We are also equally likely to pick a movie regardless of its genre, which is prone to the same problems uncovered in the previous bullet point. We will suggest movies from different genres, even if the user is only interested in one or two. This choice will also follow the general distribution of genres, so we will suggest more drama movies if more drama movies are available.

As we can see, the simplicity of our first approach comes with a few severe problems. The users may abandon the service if it suggests movies that do not match their preferences. To alleviate these issues, we suggest two refinements:

1. When making suggestions, we should consider a movie's rating, and movies with a higher rating should be more likely to be selected.

2. We should also consider genres in our selection. If a user has specified that they only like horror movies, there is little to no gain in suggesting documentaries or drama movies.

Second Approach

To mitigate some of the problems associated with the first approach, we update our selection rule based on the suggested refinements. This time around, we start by filtering all movies not labeled with the user's preferred genres. After filtering, we select the ones that have the best rating. This approach is slightly better since we only suggest highly rated movies in genres the user likes. However, there are other issues with this approach that are more subtle:

- The user might miss out on movies in other related genres. For example, there is a significant chance that they might enjoy some thriller movies, even if they have only selected horror movies as a preference.

- This approach also puts the collective opinion before the user's judgment. Since we select movies with a high rating, we might suggest a movie similar to another film that the user did not like. For example, it would probably be a poor choice to suggest *Scream 2* to a user who did not enjoy the first movie, even if most other users gave it a good rating.

Even though this approach seems better than the first one, it still has a few annoying flaws that we want to address. We need a method that puts less weight on exact genres but cares more about which movies we do and do not enjoy. To tackle this issue, we turn to the concept of *collaborative filtering*.

Final Approach

In the final approach to this problem, we ask whom we would turn to for movie recommendations before streaming services came along. We probably have a few friends that share the same taste in movies and are likely to make suggestions that we will enjoy. This idea is what collaborative filtering is all about. If person X agrees with person Y on some subject, X is more likely to share the opinion of Y on a different subject than a randomly selected person.

To make this tangible, imagine that Anna and Zoe have seen and rated the first two Scream movies, while Nick has only seen the first one. We could structure their ratings as shown in Table 7-1.

Table 7-1. *Movie ratings cast by three people*

	Scream	Scream 2
Nick	Good	?
Anna	Good	Good
Zoe	Bad	Bad

Given these ratings, who should Nick ask for advice on whether to watch *Scream 2*? The better choice is probably to ask Anna since she has the same opinion on the first movie as Nick. Since Zoe did not like *Scream*, the chances are that she has a different set of preferences and that her suggestion might not correlate that well with what Nick enjoys.

We arrive at a feasible concept for our recommender system by expanding this idea to include all service users. By doing that, recommending a movie for a user comes down to the following steps:

1. Find a certain number of users that have rated movies similar to the one asking for suggestions.

2. Compute an expected rating for all movies based on how the set of similar users have rated them.

3. Suggest the movies that have the highest expected rating.

To perform these steps, we first need to settle on how to compute the similarity of two users. We will cover two common methods in the next section. We should also note that collaborative filtering works well when there are many other users to compare to, simply because there is a greater chance that others will like the same things. However, imagine if the service only had two users who liked completely different things. The lack of data would force the algorithm to ask for suggestions from someone who likes different movies.

An alternative approach that does not rely on other users is *content-based filtering*, which focuses entirely on how the user asking for suggestions has rated other movies. This approach will not be covered in detail but may be of interest for further studies.

Similarity Measures

As the name suggests, a similarity measure is a way of determining how similar two objects are. There is an unlimited number of measures one can use, and we need to think carefully about why and how we design them. We will look at two measures here. One will not be helpful to the problem we are trying to solve, while the other is a better fit. The idea is to show how to reason about these calculations to select appropriate ones for future problems.

Cosine Similarity

The cosine similarity measures similarity by looking at the angle that separates two feature vectors. It accomplishes this by computing how well the rating vectors project onto each other. We can derive the formula for the cosine similarity between two nonzero vectors **A** and **B** from the Euclidean dot product formula.

$$\mathbf{A} \cdot \mathbf{B} = \| \mathbf{A} \| \ \| \mathbf{B} \| \cos\theta$$

$$CosSim(\mathbf{A}, \mathbf{B}) = \cos\theta = \frac{\mathbf{A} \cdot \mathbf{B}}{\| \mathbf{A} \| \ \| \mathbf{B} \|}$$

This formula yields a real number between -1 and 1 depending on how similar the two vectors are. If they point in the same general direction, the similarity score will tend toward 1. If they are opposites, the score will go toward -1. In our case, the minimum score is 0 since we cannot rate a movie with a negative number.

Now, for the sake of making these discussions tangible, suppose that four people rate two movies according to Table 7-2 on the following page.

Table 7-2. *An example of four people's ratings for two movies*

	Movie 1	Movie 2
Tyler	5	5
Sarah	5	5
Mike	5	1
Jane	1	1

Looking at these ratings, we would expect a similarity measure to say that Tyler is very similar to Sarah, a little bit similar to Mike, but not at all similar to Jane. However, running the calculations, we end up with the following results:

$$CosSim(\textbf{Tyler, Sarah}) = \frac{5 \cdot 5 + 5 \cdot 5}{\sqrt{50}\sqrt{50}} = 1$$

$$CosSim(\textbf{Tyler, Mike}) = \frac{5 \cdot 5 + 5 \cdot 1}{\sqrt{50}\sqrt{26}} = 0.832$$

$$CosSim(\textbf{Tyler, Jane}) = \frac{5 \cdot 1 + 5 \cdot 1}{\sqrt{50}\sqrt{2}} = 1$$

That is not the result we wanted. This similarity measure thinks that Tyler and Jane are just as similar as Tyler and Sarah. Let us plot the vectors to understand why. Figure 7-1 show them as arrows in a chart, where the rating Movie 1 is plotted against the X axis and Movie 2 against the Y axis.

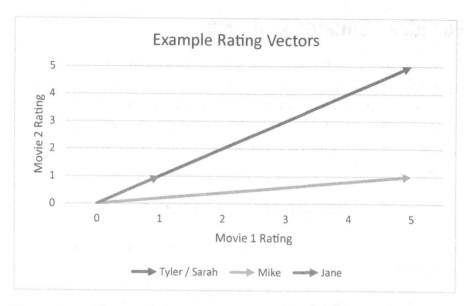

Figure 7-1. *The example ratings for Movie 1 and Movie 2 plotted as two-dimensional vectors*

The plot makes it very clear what is going on. Even though Tyler's and Sarah's ratings are very different from Jane's, the vectors they produce are parallel. Since the cosine similarity only cares about the angle between the vectors, it considers their ratings very much alike, while Mike's ratings are not entirely similar to the rest.

We will not use this similarity measure in our implementation since it does not behave the way we want. However, this example does highlight the importance of thinking about exactly how we define object similarity. A metric may seem like a decent choice at first but could end up wreaking havoc in our calculations. In this case, we could have ended up suggesting Jane's favorite movies to Tyler, which would probably have been a bad fit. Now that we have seen what can go wrong, let us define a similarity metric that works better.

Euclidean Squared Distance

The Euclidean distance, also known as the Pythagorean distance, represents a straight-line path's length between two points. By imagining each vector of movie ratings as a point, we can use this formula to compute the distance between them, ultimately measuring how similar two users are. The Euclidean distance for two column vectors, **A** and **B**, is defined as follows:

$$EucDist(A, B) = \sqrt{(A-B)^T (A-B)}$$

By using this formula to compute the similarity of our example users, we get the following:

$$EucDist(\textbf{Tyler, Sarah}) = \sqrt{(5-5)(5-5)+(5-5)(5-5)} = 0$$

$$EucDist(\textbf{Tyler, Mike}) = \sqrt{(5-5)(5-5)+(5-1)(5-1)} = 4$$

$$EucDist(\textbf{Tyler, Jane}) = \sqrt{(5-1)(5-1)+(5-1)(5-1)} = 4\sqrt{2}$$

These results look much better than the previous similarity measure. This formula also differs from the cosine similarity in that it produces larger numbers the more two vectors differ from each other. That is not a problem per se; it is just something we need to be aware of when designing our algorithm.

The Euclidean squared distance is a computationally simplified measure. It differs from the Euclidian distance only in that it does not perform the last square root calculation and so becomes

$$EucDist^2(A, B) = (A-B)^T (A-B)$$

One thing to note, and the entire reason this simplification works, is that it preserves the relative ordering of elements. Suppose that we have two numbers – x and y. Then the following holds:

$$\sqrt{x} \leq \sqrt{y} \Rightarrow x < y, \ \forall x, y \geq 0$$

The square root is a somewhat expensive operation for a computer to carry out. If we can leave it out, then we definitely will! Since two numbers will not switch their relative ordering because we leave out the square roots, we will cut some computational corners by skipping them.

Let us quickly compute the similarity between the example users, just to check out the new calculations:

$$\text{EucDist}^2 (\textbf{Tyler, Sarah}) = (5-5)(5-5) + (5-5)(5-5) = 0$$

$$\text{EucDist}^2 (\textbf{Tyler, Mike}) = (5-5)(5-5) + (5-1)(5-1) = 16$$

$$\text{EucDist}^2 (\textbf{Tyler, Jane}) = (5-1)(5-1) + (5-1)(5-1) = 32$$

That looks good. Tyler is still most similar to Sarah and least similar to Jane. However, there is still one more edge case we need to address.

Our service has an extensive collection of movies in its database. It is unlikely that all users saw all movies, and it is even less likely that they rated them all. We need to decide how to handle these calculations when some ratings are missing.

Since a 0 rating in the data marks missing ratings, no numerical issues are stopping us from computing the Euclidean squared distance as is. However, we are likely to run into some inconsistencies.

- If we compare two new users that have not had the chance to rate anything yet, the data will show zeros for all of their possible ratings. Our calculations will interpret that as the users being very similar, even though we have no idea if that is true.

- Imagine that we compare a new user, without any ratings, with two older users. Suppose that one of the older users gave all movies a 1, while the other gave all movies a 5. Our algorithm would think that the new user is more similar to the user that gave everything a rating of 1 since the Euclidean squared distance is shorter between those. However, we do not know which one is more similar.

The solution that we choose for this implementation is to interpret a missing rating as an uncertainty. If one or both users have not rated a movie, we count one of the ratings as 0 and the other as 5. This way, a missing rating will add more to the distance measure, making the users a little less similar.

Now that we know how to determine which users are similar, it is time to take on the next task. Somehow, we need to recommend movies that the user will like.

Expected Ratings

Before we head into this section, let us take a moment to remind ourselves of the structure of the ratings. A user of our service is associated with the following information:

- A unique user ID.

- A collection of ratings for all the available movies.

- A rating is an integer value between one and five. If the user has not yet rated a specific movie, it has a default rating of zero.

To compute the expected rating of a movie, we can use the formula we learned in Chapter 3:

$$\mathbb{E}[R]=\sum_{r\in R} r \cdot p(r)$$

While this formula is technically correct, we cannot simply implement it as is. The way we structure our data forces us to expand on it slightly to make rational calculations. Let us start with a modification that does not directly impact the mathematical formulation but rather the computation of probabilities for each rating.

Laplace Smoothing

Let us look at the distribution of all ratings for the movie *Big Fish*, shown in Figure 7-2. This distribution comes from the ratings of all 800 users available in our data set.

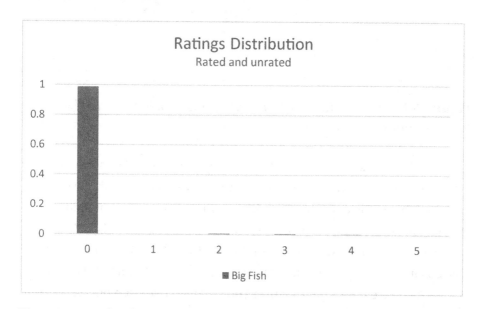

Figure 7-2. *The distribution of all ratings for the movie Big Fish*

As we can see, most of the users did not yet rate this movie. To be precise, 98.6% of all users have yet to provide a rating for *Big Fish*. This observation is important because it will prove helpful at a later step. However, for now, let us focus on the users that did rate the movie. Figure 7-3 shows the bars associated with the users that did provide a rating.

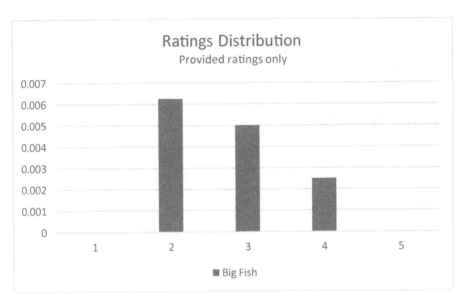

Figure 7-3. *The distribution of ratings for Big Fish, without the unrated marker category*

This chart makes it much easier to see what is going on. Most of our users seem to have gone somewhere in the middle. Not one single user has rated the movie a one or a five. If we were to run these probabilities through our algorithm, we would essentially tell it that there is a 0% probability that a user would ever rank it anything but two, three, or four. It is reasonable to believe that someone could provide a rating of one and that we just have not found that user yet. We need to design our algorithm so that there is always a nonzero probability for all ratings. Enter Laplace smoothing.

The idea of Laplace smoothing is to skew the distribution a little bit toward the uniform distribution. It does so by adding a *pseudocount*, which is why we sometimes refer to the method as *Additive Smoothing*. Adding a pseudocount to each sample point ensures that all of them end up with a nonzero probability. Let us look at an example to make the concept more understandable.

Imagine that we roll a die ten times and that Table 7-3 shows the number of times we land on a specific number.

Table 7-3. *Counting the outcomes of ten die rolls*

Outcome	Count
1	2
2	3
3	2
4	0
5	2
6	1

It looks like we got plenty of twos in this round but did not get a single four. If we were to approximate the probabilities of each outcome, we would end up with the following results:

$$P[X=1]=\frac{2}{10}=0.2$$

$$P[X=2]=\frac{3}{10}=0.3$$

$$P[X=3]=\frac{2}{10}=0.2$$

$$P[X=4]=\frac{0}{10}=0.0$$

$$P[X=5]=\frac{2}{10}=0.2$$

$$P[X=6]=\frac{1}{10}=0.1$$

In earlier chapters, we computed the true probability of any face on a fair die to be approximately 16.66%, so some of these results are way off. Our approximations suggest 30% of getting a two, while there is no way we will ever roll a four. In the case of a die roll, we could easily repeat the experiment more times and gather more information. However, in the case of movie reviews, that is not as simple. Since we have 2000 movies and only 800 users, there is a significant chance that one or more ratings will have a zero count on most movies. We say that the data is *sparse*.

To mitigate this issue, imagine adding a pseudocount of 1 to each outcome in Table 7-3. We now have a total of 16 data points, which yields the following new probabilities:

$$P[X=1]=\frac{3}{16}=0.1875$$

$$P[X=2]=\frac{4}{16}=0.25$$

$$P[X=3]=\frac{3}{16}=0.1875$$

$$P[X=4]=\frac{1}{16}=0.0625$$

$$P[X=5]=\frac{3}{16}=0.1875$$

$$P[X=6]=\frac{2}{16}=0.125$$

With the pseudocount, we no longer think that rolling a four is an impossibility. In fact, if we were to add an infinite pseudocount to the outcomes in Table 7-3, our results would tend toward the true distribution. However, most distributions are not uniform. That means we cannot add a massive number to each movie rating and expect good things to happen. We will settle for a pseudocount of one. That is enough to eradicate zero probabilities while not skewing the original distribution too much.

Rating Probabilities

We just developed a strategy for handling the zero probabilities that often show up in sparse data. Let us now look at an approach to approximating the probability of a rating. Remember that we formulated the expected rating using the following formula:

$$\mathbb{E}[R] = \sum_{r \in R} r \cdot p(r)$$

We want to focus on the term *p(r)* here. Imagine that a movie receives a single rating, a four. Using the Laplace smoothing technique we just learned about, we would approximate the probability of each rating by the following calculations:

$$p(0) = \frac{1}{7} \approx 0.1429$$

$$p(1) = \frac{1}{7} \approx 0.1429$$

$$p(2) = \frac{1}{7} \approx 0.1429$$

$$p(3) = \frac{1}{7} \approx 0.1429$$

$$p(4) = \frac{2}{7} \approx 0.2857$$

$$p(5) = \frac{1}{7} \approx 0.1429$$

These results look well and good, but there is a subtle problem that we need to address. Our definition of a rating does not correspond to the way we structure the data. Remember that a zero rating is just a placeholder meaning that a user did not rate the movie in question. In this case, we are actually diluting the probability of each rating by including the non-ratings.

To solve this issue, we will lean on Reverend Bayes and his theorem. Remember that we state Bayes' Theorem as follows:

$$P[A|B] = \frac{P[B|A] \cdot P[A]}{P[B]}$$

Since we are looking for the probability of a rating given that the rating is greater than zero, we can use Bayes' Theorem to make the following formulation:

$$P[r|r>0] \cdot P[r>0] = P[r>0|r] \cdot P[r]$$

By massaging this equation, we can isolate the term we are really interested in, namely, $p(r \mid r > 0)$:

$$P[r|r>0] = \frac{P[r>0|r] \cdot P[r]}{P[r>0]}$$

The preceding equation is the probability we really want – the probability of a rating given that it is a real rating and not a placeholder. Let us analyze each of the right-hand terms individually to see what it takes to compute each of them.

- P(r > 0 | r): This term will be one for all real ratings because it is certain that the rating is greater than zero if it is not a placeholder. By the same logic, it will be zero for all the placeholders. Since the placeholder itself is zero, we can drop this term from the equation. It will not make a difference in either of the cases.

- P(r): This term is the probability approximation we get from the Laplace smoothing. We have a way of computing this proportion for all movies based on the data.

- P(r > 0): The probability that a rating is greater than zero is also available from the Laplace smoothing. Either we sum the probabilities of all ratings above zero, or we subtract the probability of zero from one.

Given this reasoning, we can rewrite the formula for an expected rating to the following:

$$\mathbb{E}[R] = \sum_{r \in R} r \cdot p(r \mid r > 0) = \sum_{r \in R} r \cdot \frac{p(r)}{p(r > 0)}$$

There it is. We have arrived at a formulation that lets us compute an expected rating. With the help of the similarity measure and Laplace smoothing, we are ready to implement a movie recommendation algorithm.

Implementing the Algorithm

This section will cover a Swift implementation of the recommendation algorithm we just derived in this chapter. We will also get to know a new module from the Accelerate framework. Instead of using CBLAS and LAPACK to do linear algebra, we will visit the *vDSP* API. vDSP provides functionality relating to digital signal processing and scientific data processing. It offers tools for working with vectors, Fourier transforms, convolution, and many other tasks.

The Main Program

Before getting into the details, let us look at the main program to acquaint ourselves with the general structure. Listing 7-1 shows the implementation.

Listing 7-1. The main program of our recommender system.

```
var raters = DataLoader.load(
  MovieWatcher.self,
  from: .movieRatings
)

let user = raters.remove(at: 0)

let recommendations = MovieRecommender
  .recommend(
    movies: 5,
    for: user,
    from: raters,
    neighbors: 30
  )
```

As per usual, we start by loading the data set into memory and decoding it into Swift types that we can use. The MovieWatcher type consists of a user ID, an array of movie ratings, and an array of corresponding movie titles, as shown in Listing 7-2.

We remove and store away the first user in the collection of movie enthusiasts. We placed this user first because they have a very nice and clean set of genre preferences, namely, comedy and horror. That way, we have a chance to verify that the recommendations we receive on the other end are reasonable.

After separating the user looking for recommendations from the rest, we call into the MovieRecommender and ask it to suggest five movies based on the methods covered in this chapter. The result is an array of strings containing recommended movie titles.

Listing 7-2. The definition of the MovieWatcher type

```
struct MovieWatcher {
  let id: Int
  let titles: [String]
  let ratings: [Double]
}
```

To complete the task at hand, the MovieRecommender needs to determine which 30 users are most similar to the one asking for suggestions. We call these 30 users for *neighbors* since that is a common term when looking for close-by data points in this manner.

The recommender also needs to compute the Laplace smoothed rating distribution from those neighbors, calculate the expected rating for each movie, and return a requested number of titles for which those expectations are highest. Listing 7-3 shows the implementation of the method recommend(movies:for:from:neighbors:).

Listing 7-3. The implementation of recommend(movies:for:from:neighbors:)

```
func recommend(
  movies: Int,
  for someone: MovieWatcher,
  from others: [MovieWatcher],
  neighbors: Int
) -> [String] {
```

```
let similarUsers = getMostSimilar(
  to: someone,
  from: others,
  neighbors: neighbors
)

let ratingDist = ratingDistributions(
  from: similarUsers,
  movieCount: someone.ratings.count,
  neighbors: neighbors
)

let expectations = expectedRatings(
  using: ratingDist
)

return getTopRated(
  movies: movies,
  for: someone,
  expectations: expectations
)
}
```

Like in Chapter 6, we split the different subproblems into helper functions. This approach makes for better readability and understanding of what recommend(movies:for:from:neighbors:) does. The first step is to compute the 30 most similar users, which we delegate to getMostSimilar(to:from:neighbors:). Listing 7-4 shows the implementation of that method.

Listing 7-4. The implementation of getMostSimilar(to:from: neighbors:)

```
private static func getMostSimilar(
  to someone: MovieWatcher,
  from others: [MovieWatcher],
  neighbors: Int
) -> [MovieWatcher] {

  let similarities = others
    .map { other in
      similarity(lhs: someone, rhs: other)
    }

  let mostSimilar = similarities
    .enumerated()
    .sorted { lhs, rhs in
      lhs.element < rhs.element
    }
    .dropLast(others.count - neighbors)
    .map { offset, element in
      others[offset]
    }

  return mostSimilar
}
```

We start by mapping all users to their respective similarity measures. We use the Euclidean squared distance we talked about earlier and will discuss the implementation in a moment.

Once we have all similarities, we bundle them with their respective array index by calling enumerated() and sort them in ascending order according to the similarity value. Remember that the more similar two users are, the smaller the similarity value will be. Finally, we drop all but the first neighbor's similarities and map them back to their corresponding user. This operation leaves us with an array containing the most similar number of users, which we return to the calling function.

To fully understand this function, we need to look at the method similarity(lhs:rhs:). Listing 7-5 shows the implementation.

Listing 7-5. Our implementation of the method similarity(lhs:rhs:)

```
func similarity(
  lhs: MovieWatcher,
  rhs: MovieWatcher
) -> Double {

  var (left, right) = (lhs.ratings, rhs.ratings)

  for index in 0 ..< left.count {
    if left[index] == 0 {
      right[index] = 5
    } else if right[index] == 0 {
      left[index] = 5
    }
  }

  return vDSP
    .distanceSquared(
      left,
      right
    )
}
```

This function contains two interesting parts. First, it fetches the two users' rating collections. Remember that we wanted missing ratings to decrease the similarity between two users. Therefore, the algorithm sets the two ratings to zero and five for all movies where at least one rating is missing, making the distance contribution as large as possible.

Finally, we make use of the vDSP module for the first time. We show the definition of distanceSquared(_:_:) in Listing 7-6 for reference.

Listing 7-6. The definition of vDSP.distanceSquared(_:_:)

```
static func distanceSquared<U, V>(
  _ pointA: U,
  _ pointB: V
) -> Double
where U : AccelerateBuffer,
      V : AccelerateMutableBuffer,
      U.Element == Double,
      V.Element == Double
```

Since there are a lot of generics and constraints going on, we will try to break down the most important things to know. First of all, the method takes two vectors as arguments. The vectors represent the two points that we want to use for our calculations. They are constrained by the requirement that they need to conform to the AccelerateBuffer and AccelerateMutableBuffer protocols. They are also constrained such that the elements inside the vectors need to be of the type Double. Upon completion, this method returns the Euclidean squared distance between the provided points.

Now that we have extracted the most similar users, we can calculate the distribution of different ratings for each movie. The ratingDistributi ons(from:movieCount:neighbors:) method uses the Laplace smoothing technique to approximate the distribution of ratings for each of the available movies. Listing 7-7 shows the implementation.

Listing 7-7. Computing the rating distributions for each movie

```swift
func ratingDistributions(
  from similarUsers: [MovieWatcher],
  movieCount: Int,
  neighbors: Int
) -> [[Double]] {

  let N = neighbors.realValue
  let pseudoCount = 1.0
  let numRatings = 6
  let total = N + numRatings.realValue * pseudoCount

  let columns = [Double](
    repeating: pseudoCount,
    count: numRatings
  )

  let ratingMatrix = [[Double]](
    repeating: columns,
    count: movieCount
  )

  let counts = similarUsers
    .reduce(into: ratingMatrix) { matrix, user in
      user.ratings
        .enumerated()
        .forEach { movie, rating in
          matrix[movie][Int(rating)] += 1
        }
    }

  return counts
    .map { movieRatings in
```

```
movieRatings.map { rating in
  rating / total
}
}
}
```

In the first couple of lines, we determine the size of our pseudocount and compute the total number of data points we will have for each movie after counting. We create a matrix with one row for each movie and one column for each rating between zero and five. Using the same enumeration trick as before, we can track which movie receives a specific rating and increment the corresponding counter. Finally, we turn the counts into proportions by dividing by the total number of data points we computed at the top of the function.

When this method returns, it hands back a matrix that specifies the approximated probabilities that a movie receives some rating. We base these probabilities on the neighbors we computed earlier, so they should somewhat represent how the user requesting suggestions could rate each movie. Now that we have distributions to work with, we are finally ready to compute an expected rating for each movie. Listing 7-8 shows the implementation of expectedRatings(using:), which handles this task for us.

Listing 7-8. Calculating an expected rating for each movie in the collection

```
func expectedRatings(
  using ratingsDist: [[Double]]
) -> [Double] {

  ratingsDist
    .map { distribution -> Double in
      let bayesDenom = 1 - distribution[0]
```

```
    return distribution
      .enumerated()
      .dropFirst()
      .reduce(into: 0.0) { expectation, args in
        let (intRating, prob) = args
        let rating = intRating.realValue
        expectation += rating * prob / bayesDenom
      }
  }
}
```

The program iterates over the arrays holding the rating distribution for each movie. For each distribution, we compute the term $p(r > 0)$ and store it in the variable named bayesDenom. We use the enumeration trick to get each rating along with the probability, drop the first entry since that contains the placeholder for non-ratings, and compute the expected value using the formula we derived earlier.

This function produces an array of real numbers, one for each movie. Each number represents the expected rating of a movie as determined by the most similar users. This collection of expected values should roughly represent how the user we are making recommendations for would rate each movie. All that remains is to extract the top-rated movies and return their names. Listing 7-9 shows getTopRated(movies:for:expectations:), which performs this last step and completes the movie recommendation task.

Listing 7-9. Mapping the top expected ratings to a collection of recommended movies

```
private static func getTopRated(
  movies: Int,
  for someone: MovieWatcher,
  expectations: [Double]
```

```
) -> [String] {

  expectations
    .enumerated()
    .sorted { lhs, rhs in
      if someone.ratings[lhs.offset] != 0 {
        return false
      }
      if someone.ratings[rhs.offset] != 0 {
        return true
      }
      return lhs.element > rhs.element
    }
    .dropLast(expectations.count - movies)
    .map { index, _ in
      someone.titles[index]
    }
}
```

Most of the stages in this processing pipeline should look familiar by now. The enumeration pairs each expected rating to the index of the movie it describes. However, the sorting stage does something that is not immediately obvious. Even though a movie may have an excellent expected rating, we do not want to suggest it if the user has already rated it. So instead of sorting only on the expected values, we add two conditions that place already rated movies further down the list.

Once we have finished sorting, we drop all but the first movie ratings and map them back to their respective titles. These two stages produce an array of movie titles that we can return to the main program and display to the user. Listing 7-10 shows us printing the recommendations in the main program.

Listing 7-10. Printing the suggested movies for the user with ID 1

```
print(
    """
    Recommended movies for user \(user.id):

    \(
        recommendations
            .joined(separator: "\n")
    )

    """
)

// Prints:
// Recommended movies for user 1:
//
// Dawn Patrol
// Surfer, Dude
// Winnie Mandela
// Grand Theft Parsons
// An American in Hollywood
```

We have some movie suggestions! We know that the user we wanted suggestions for was a fan of comedies and horror movies, so let us assess how reasonable these recommendations are. Table 7-4 shows the genres of each suggested movie.

Table 7-4. *The suggested movies and their genres*

Movie	Genres
Dawn Patrol	Thriller/Drama
Surfer, Dude	Comedy
Winnie Mandela	History/Drama
Grand Theft Parsons	Comedy/Drama
An American in Hollywood	Comedy/Drama

These results look pretty decent. There are quite a few comedies in the suggestions. One thriller, we could argue, is related to the horror genre in some sense.

The only movie that does not immediately fit into the user's genre preferences is Winnie Mandela, which is a drama movie. However, these movies were all suggested by others who like many of the same movies that our user does. It may be a good match, even if the genres do not line up perfectly. Remember that the idea of this type of collaborative filtering is to look at the perceived quality of a movie inside a group of like-minded people. Since genres are not as important, we may end up with suggestions that cross the boundaries of genre preferences but that a user could still enjoy.

Table 7-5 lists a few other user indices and what their preferred genres are. Feel free to play around with the code project and see what suggestions the algorithm generates.

Table 7-5. *Some other user indices and their preferred genres*

User Index	Preferred Genres
8	Action
54	Comedy, Mystery
82	Drama, Fantasy
172	Comedy, Romance
220	Animation

Chapter Summary

This chapter weaved together many of the concepts we have looked at throughout this book. We learned how to solve a real-world problem step by step by incorporating ideas and concepts that build on statistical analysis. We covered two ways of measuring similarity and discussed how they work and how they may perform poorly on certain kinds of data. We also talked about the application of expected values and revisited Bayes' Theorem to derive a formula that would help us achieve our goal.

The implementation part of the chapter went over the code needed to recommend movie titles based on existing knowledge. We got to work with chains of higher-order functions and see how they can form a declarative flow from input to desired output. We also got a quick introduction to the vDSP module, which contains several helpful methods when working with vectors. Since vDSP is a part of the Accelerate framework, these methods will speed up execution by computing our results on the CPU's vector processor.

The next chapter wraps things up by summarizing what we have learned throughout this book. It also looks at some of the many fields where it is beneficial to know about statistical methods and suggests resources and interesting related topics for future studies.

CHAPTER 8

Reflections

This book has presented new topics, techniques, and frameworks at a rapid pace. To fully digest new material, it is essential to take the time to reflect on what we have done. This chapter will walk through the most important topics of the previous chapters and provide repetition and some time to reflect on how the different subjects fit together. Before we wrap up, we will also look at some professions where knowledge of statistical analysis is crucial and suggest related topics for further studies.

The Swift Programming Language

In Chapter 1, we discussed Swift and its viability as a statistical analysis tool. As we mentioned then, there are plenty of good alternatives, such as Python and R, for solving these types of problems. Swift does, however, have advantages in some situations and should not be excluded from the toolbox just because there are other languages available.

- Swift is a statically typed and compiled language, making it fast and efficient when dealing with large-scale data.

- Plenty of frameworks and libraries are available via the Swift Package Manager, providing access to a vast landscape of tools upon which to build.

J. Andersson, *Statistical Analysis with Swift*, https://doi.org/10.1007/978-1-4842-7765-2_8

- Swift is also the primary language for Apple platforms,
  making it easier to incorporate our algorithms into
  applications on Macs, iPhones, and iPads. This point
  is important on its own because, in the end, we want
  customers to be able to enjoy the results of our work.

This book worked with data stored in CSV files. The main reason
for this was the balance between readability and storage requirements.
We also presented a few other formats used for data persistence, such
as *JSON, XML,* and *Protobuf.* These are all formats that can be easily
written to and read from a file. However, Swift has several options to use
more sophisticated database management systems to store and retrieve
data. There is even the possibility to choose between relational, NoSQL,
and graph based. Table 8-1 shows a few of the options available to Swift
developers. Given all these different possibilities, we are sure to find a good
match for our use case, no matter what it might be.

Table 8-1. *Database management systems available to Swift developers*

Name	Type
SQLite	Relational DBMS
Realm	NoSQL DBMS
ObjectBox	NoSQL DBMS
Neo4j	Graph DBMS

We have been using many of Swift's built-in language features
throughout this book, such as higher-order functions and KeyPath types.
Higher-order functions have played a prominent role in pretty much
all of our code projects. Methods such as filter(_:), reduce(_:), and
map(_:) have helped us transform and refine our data sets until we arrive
at the final result. KeyPath types helped make some of our algorithms

more generic by allowing the calling function to select one or more target variables. That approach allowed us to make truly versatile programs and, for example, quickly change which variables to use for our linear regression computations.

Another valuable feature of Swift is that we get access to a world of data coders through the `Encodable` and `Decodable` protocols. Some are handed to us by Apple, others by talented third-party developers. Almost no matter what data format we use, we can be sure that there are plenty of options to parse data files that do not require us to disassemble them by hand.

Probability Theory

In Chapter 2, we covered some of the most important concepts in probability theory. We learned that even though it may seem like a niche topic, most of us encounter it daily. We list some examples of real-world applications here:

- The weather forecast may tell us that there is a 5% chance of rain tomorrow.

- A public opinion survey may show that a presidential candidate gained 2% over their opponent but may also conclude that the result is not statistically significant.

- Records show that 85% of a country's population received a vaccine dose against a new disease and that 50% of people getting hospitalized are unvaccinated.

The last example is a perfect candidate for using another essential idea we learned about – Bayes' Theorem. Using Bayes' Rule, we could, for example, calculate the probability of ending up in the hospital given that we got vaccinated. This seemingly simple formula provides a powerful tool to weigh different scenarios against each other by infusing more information into our estimates.

Chapter 2 also taught us about independence and how it often simplifies our computations. Some may argue that everything is interconnected and that two events can never truly be independent of each other. However, if two events' effect on each other's probabilities is acceptably small, we often say they are independent either way. One of the reasons is that we like simplicity, and it is less complicated to think about things that do not interact. Another reason is that if the effect is sufficiently small, we will still end up with an approximation close to the true value, so we do not give up much accuracy.

Distributions

While learning about sample spaces, we got some insight into how to categorize them depending on the nature of their sample points. This way of looking at possible outcomes led us to discuss discrete and continuous distributions and their properties.

A discrete distribution is characterized by its probability mass function (PMF), while a continuous distribution has a probability density function (PDF). Both of these describe the likelihood of all the sample points contained by the distribution. However, we also learned that only the PMF yields a number that we can interpret as a probability. The PDF, on the other hand, gives a relative likelihood value. Sample points that are more likely get a higher number, but we need to compute an integral to get a proper probability. We also learned that the probability of a single sample point in a continuous distribution is zero and that we should compute probabilities over ranges of sample points.

Another function that helps us describe distributions is the *cumulative distribution function* (CDF). It tells us the probability that a sample falls at or below a specified point. For example, the CDF of a standard normal distribution would tell us that there is a 50% chance that a random sample is lesser than or equal to zero.

Chapter 3 also introduced the idea of expected values. The most common expected value is the average. We compute it by weighting each sample point by its probability in a given distribution. However, there are also other expected values, such as the distribution's variance, skewness, and kurtosis. We covered the variance and the closely related standard deviation in our studies. However, the other two properties are easy to look up and understand since they build on the same concept.

Regression Techniques

Chapter 4 guided us through both simple and multiple linear regression. On the way, we learned about a range of related methods.

- Linear interpolation and extrapolation from two data points are helpful if we believe an exact linear relationship between two properties exists. One example used in the chapter was the relationship between weight and cost when purchasing apples. If one pound of apples costs $1.3, it is reasonable to believe that two pounds will cost us $2.6.

- Linear splines can be useful when we have irregular data points that show a linear tendency. We can then interpolate between the available data points to approximate any value between them. However, we also learned that this method has shortcomings, such as the need to store a complete data set and the fact that our estimates can diverge from the true values quickly if we try to approximate values outside the range of our original data.

- Linear regression tries to strike a sweet spot between the previous two methods. It only requires that we store the coefficients for a linear equation, and it generalizes the overall trend of the original data. The former implies that we do not need much storage space to make estimates once we have the coefficients. The latter, in turn, reduces the problems we saw that splines could have outside of the range where we have empirical data.

To construct the formula and algorithm for linear regression, we also learned about loss functions. Loss functions are by no means unique to linear regression. We use them in many exciting applications, such as machine learning algorithms, where there is a need to approximate functions.

Chapter 4 also introduced us to the Accelerate framework and the BLAS and LAPACK libraries. All of these provide excellent tools when working with mathematical computations that involve linear algebra. The fact that the computer can parallelize much of the work saves a massive amount of time compared to computing everything serially. We only covered the minuscule functionality we needed for our specific use case, but these libraries contain an ocean of valuable mathematical functions at our disposal. Feel free to dive further into the documentation referenced in Chapter 4 to discover more.

Hypothesis Testing

As we stated at the beginning of Chapter 5, hypothesis testing is one of the topics that students find most challenging to understand. Just the task of identifying the null and alternative hypotheses may be difficult.

- The null hypothesis, H_0, suggests that the currently accepted truth still holds. For example, if previous studies have shown that Michigan's average temperature is 64.6°F in April, then H_0 states it still is.

- The alternative hypothesis, H_A, states a new assumption we want to test. If we believe that Michigan has become warmer in recent years, H_A states that the average temperature is greater than 64.6°F.

To start testing, we needed to find out more about the distribution of sample means. As we use more and more samples for our calculations, the sample mean tends more and more toward the true mean. However, unless we use the entire population, there is a non-negligible likelihood that our calculation is off by some amount. To put a number on the uncertainty, we turn to the Central Limit Theorem, which tells us that a normal distribution can approximate the distribution of sample means. This theorem holds regardless of which distribution the samples come from, given that we have enough samples.

Learning how to estimate the uncertainty in our computations allowed us to determine cutoff points where the alternative hypothesis was unlikely enough to have happened by random chance. The cutoffs led us to define confidence levels, alpha values, and p-values, which are important tools when quantifying how uncertain a result is. Including these values lets others decide whether or not to act on the results.

Statistical Methods for Data Compression

Statistical methods are not exclusive to heavy data science tasks or machine learning algorithms. In Chapter 6, we learned that we could use them in more traditional computer science topics like data compression. To start, we had to learn about functions.

- Surjective functions behave such that we can reach all elements in the range. However, multiple domain members can map to the same range element. Because of this, we may not be able to determine a unique mapping back to the domain.

- Injective functions map all domain members to unique elements in the range. This behavior is nice since there is a unique way to map those elements back to their respective domain member. However, there may be elements in the range that are unreachable from the domain. This drawback means that we cannot guarantee an inverse mapping from the range to the domain exists.

- Bijective functions are both surjective and injective, which means that all domain members map a unique element in the range, and all range members are reachable. When both of these properties apply, we know that our function has an inverse. We can use this pair of functions to develop lossless compression algorithms.

Apart from bijection, we also introduced the concept of "approximate bijection." While this is not a commonly accepted term, it appropriately describes the idea of lossy functions, where the inverse is not guaranteed to map a range member back to the original domain element. Instead, it maps back to some member in its proximity.

To implement a compression algorithm, we needed some bijective function to shrink and expand our data. In our case, we learned about Huffman codes and how to create them using Huffman trees. Thanks to the theory behind Huffman codes, we managed to design an algorithm that significantly shrank a text file and later decompressed it back to its original form. During the implementation, we also got hands-on experience using some of Swift's more low-level functionalities, such as bitwise operators and pointer types. We also got to see some more general computer science conventions, such as memory alignment. These conventions serve their purposes well, but they also force us to think about how to structure our data when packing it. In connection to this, we also suggested an exercise related to improving the algorithm's way of packing and unpacking bytes.

Statistical Methods in Recommender Systems

In Chapter 7, we introduced a very current topic – recommender systems. Since most services use some sort of algorithm to suggest content or products, it is vital to have experience with some basic ideas behind them. However, it also allowed us to mix and match some of the theoretical elements we learned throughout the book.

We learned about similarity measures and how they provide a way to group data points depending on some notion of likeness. However, one similarity measure does not fit all problems, which we became painfully aware of as we tried to determine the similarity of movie enthusiasts by the cosine similarity. The section gave some intuition about what we need to think about when selecting a measure for our particular use case.

We saw how Bayes' Theorem could help us overcome limitations in representing our data points. In the end, we used it to derive a version of the expected value formula that better fit our needs. Our algorithm became much easier to implement thanks to the mathematical gymnastics we performed.

During the implementation stage, we got acquainted with yet another module from the Accelerate framework named vDSP. This module provides functionality for performing computations with vectors and, as the name suggests, digital signal processing. Like with BLAS and LAPACK, we only used a tiny fraction of the available functionality. There are still plenty of practical methods to discover for those that are interested.

Note   Apple's documentation provides a good starting point for those who want to dive deeper into the Accelerate framework. Visit https://developer.apple.com/documentation/accelerate to learn more.

Professional Areas of Application

Now that we have opened the door to using Swift as a tool for statistical analysis, it is reasonable to ask where this knowledge is applicable. The following list provides a glimpse at the different areas where statistical analysis is a relevant skill, but it is not, by any measure, complete. There are plenty of professions that benefit from these skills, and the future will likely bring even more job titles where it serves us well to know these concepts.

Data Scientist

The obvious first choice is, of course, the data scientist role. Data scientists work with large amounts of data, building mathematical models and computer programs that provide useful information about trends, behaviors, or new revenue opportunities.

Machine Learning Engineer

Machine learning engineers are skilled programmers who research, design, or implement complex software. They work with massive data sets to develop algorithms that can learn and make decisions or predictions.

Data Engineer

Data engineers work much more on the computer science side than, for example, data scientists. Still, it is relevant for them to know their way around statistics when they build systems to collect, store, and analyze vast amounts of data.

Data Analyst

Data analysts take on more of a customer-facing role than the previous professions. Their job is to collect, analyze, and interpret data and present the findings so that all relevant stakeholders can absorb it and use it to make appropriate decisions.

Topics for Further Studies

Learning is a nice blend of joy and frustration. The feeling of finally getting something and applying it in practice is one of the main reasons we continue to learn. However, sometimes it is difficult to know where to look for the next challenge. After all, if we never learned that something exists, it is nearly impossible to look for it. If you enjoyed the topics in this book, this list provides some related areas that may be of interest. Whichever one you pick for your next undertaking, I wish you all the best on your journey toward more knowledge.

Numerical Linear Algebra

This book has gone through a fair share of linear algebra and worked with BLAS, LAPACK, and the Accelerate framework. If those sections were exciting, further studies in numerical linear algebra might be of interest. *Khan Academy* offers an excellent course in linear algebra, and Grant Sanderson's *3Blue1Brown* provides a very intuitive video series on the essentials.

Multivariate Statistics

This book has mainly concerned itself with looking at a single variable, so-called univariate statistics. However, the complexity of data today often requires the analysis of multiple variables. *An Introduction to Multivariate Statistical Analysis* by Theodore W. Anderson is a good place to start for those who want to dive deeper.

Supervised Machine Learning

Machine learning is a hot topic at the moment, and the fact is that the linear regression we implemented earlier counts as supervised machine learning. Those interested in learning more about these techniques and picking up a new programming language may want to check out *Python Machine Learning* by Sebastian Raschka.

Index

A, B

Bayes' Theorem, 31, 33, 201, 207
BLAS and LAPACK libraries, 204
BLAS function, 96, 97

C

Cumulative distribution
function (CDF), 48, 49, 58,
60, 69, 202
Central Limit Theorem, 117, 118,
134, 205
Chi-squared tests, 134
CodableCSV, 9
Collaborative filtering, 169, 171
Continuous distribution
definition, 55
expected value, 67
exponential, 59, 60, 62
normal, 62, 64–66
PDF, 55–58
variance/standard deviation,
68, 69

D

Data analysts, 209
Data compression

compression stage, 145–149,
151, 153, 154, 156
decompression stage, 158–162,
164, 165
function behaviors, 136–138
Huffman coding, 141
lossless *vs*. lossy, 139, 140
statistical methods, 205, 206
Data engineers, 208
Data scientists, 2, 117, 208
Decompression, 135, 136, 139, 144,
147, 158, 164
Discrete distribution
applications, 53–55
Bernoulli trial, 41–43
binomial, 49–51, 53
Distribution
continuous, 40
definition, 39
discrete random
variable, 40
probabilities, 40
Domain, 75, 78, 79, 136
Dot-dot-dot syntax, 91

E, F

Exponential distribution, 59–61,
64, 66

J. Andersson, *Statistical Analysis with Swift*, https://doi.org/10.1007/978-1-4842-7765-2

G

General Addition Rule, 23, 25–27

H

Higher-order functions, 14, 17,
    19, 178
Huffman algorithm
  binary tree, 142
  code, 143
  definition, 141
  frequencies, 141
  requirements, 141
  storing, 144
Hypothesis testing
  alpha values, 124
  alternative hypothesis, 111
  central limit theorem, 117, 119,
    121, 122
  confidence levels, 123
  definition, 109
  null hypothesis, 111
  performing test, 124, 125
  p-value, 126, 127, 129
  sample means, 114, 115, 117
  standardization
    chi-square test, 134
    computing confidence
      intervals, 132, 133
    standard score, 130–132
  tails, 112, 113
  tools, 123
  WAIS, 110

I, J, K

Invertible Matrix Theorem, 90, 100

L

Linear regression
  definition, 71
  implementation, 81–85
  inter-or extrapolation, 72
  loss function, 76, 77, 79
  multiple, 86, 91–94, 96–98, 100,
    102–106
  optimal solution, 79, 80
  predicting house sale
    prices, 107
  spline, 73, 74
  techniques, 75
  vectors, 87, 89, 90

M, N

Mutually exclusive
    events, 22–24, 26
Machine learning
    engineers, 208
Multiple linear regression, 86, 97,
    98, 203
Multivariate Statistical
    Analysis, 210

O

One-tailed test, 113

P, Q

Probability density
function (PDF), 55
parseTree(_:) function, 160
predict(x:) function, 82
Probability
Baye's theorem, 31, 32
conditional, 27–30
event, 20, 22
General Addition Rule, 23–27
independence, 31
sample spaces, 21
Probability density function (PDF),
55, 69, 202
Probability mass function (PMF),
44, 202
Probability theory, 21, 201
Pythagorean distance, 176

R

Random variables
discrete *vs.* continuous, 35–37
example, 34, 35
single capital letter, 34
Recommender system
approaching problems,
169–172
cosine similarity measures,
173–175
definition, 167
Euclidean distance, 176, 177
examples, 167, 168

expected ratings
laplace smoothing, 179–182
rating probabilities, 183, 184
service, 178
functions, 168
implementation
getMostSimilar(to:from:
neighbors:), 188, 189
main program, 186
movie suggestions, 197
MovieWatcher type, 187, 188
preferred genres, 198
rating distributions, 191,
193–195
method
similarity(lhs:rhs:), 190
services, 207

S, T

Statistical methods, 135, 198
Statistics and probability
theory, 21
Supervised machine
learning, 210
Swift
Apple platforms, 200
code repository, 7
correctness, 3
database management
systems, 200
data formats, 5, 6
decodable protocol, 7–10

Swift (*cont.*)
  definition, 1, 199
  hardware acceleration, 4
  higher-order functions, 14, 16
  KeyPath type, 10–13, 17
  performance, 2
  safety, 2
Swift Package Manager, 4–6, 199

U, V

Univariate statistics, 210

W

Wechsler Adult Intelligence
    Scale (WAIS), 109
withUnsafeBytes(_:) method, 159

X, Y

XTransX, 94, 102

Z

Z-score, 130–132

Printed in the United States
by Baker & Taylor Publisher Services

Printed in the United States
by Baker & Taylor Publisher Services